COMPLETE
CAT CARE

COMPLETE
CAT CARE

LONDON, NEW YORK, MELBOURNE,
MUNICH, AND DELHI

DORLING KINDERSLEY
Senior Editor Sam Atkinson
Project Art Editor Amy Child
Jacket Designer Laura Brim
Jacket Editor Manisha Majithia
Jacket Design Development Manager Sophia Tampakopoulos
Producer, Pre-Production Rachel Ng
Producer Mary Slater
Photographer Gary Ombler
Managing Editor Esther Ripley
Managing Art Editor Karen Self
Publisher Sarah Larter
Art Director Phil Ormerod
Associate Publishing Director Liz Wheeler
Publishing Director Jonathan Metcalf

Consultant Alison Logan
Contributors Ann Baggaley, Katie John, Jenna Kiddie

DK INDIA
Senior Editor Monica Saigal
Editor Antara Moitra
Senior Art Editor Chhaya Sajwan
Art Editor Supriya Mahajan, Devan Das
Assitant Art Editor Ankita Mukherjee, Namita, Payal Rosalind Malik
Managing Editor Pakshalika Jayaprakash
Managing Art Editor Arunesh Talapatra
DTP Designers Bimlesh Tiwary, Jagtar Singh, Mohammad Usman
Pre-Production Manager Balwant Singh
Production Manager Pankaj Sharma
Picture Researcher Surya Sankash Sarangi

First published in Great Britain in 2014
by Dorling Kindersley Limited, 80 Strand, London WC2R ORL
A Penguin Random House Company

Copyright © 2014 Dorling Kindersley Limited

10 9 8 7 6 5 4 3 2
002 – 192886 – Feb/2014

A CIP catalogue record for this book is available from the British Library.

ISBN 978-1-4093-4638-8

Printed and bound in China by Hung Hing

Discover more at
www.dk.com

Disclaimer
Every effort has been made to ensure that the information in this book is accurate.
Neither the publishers nor the authors accept any legal responsibility for any personal
injury or injuries to cats or other damage or loss arising from the undertaking of any of
the activities presented in this book, or from the reliance on any advice in this book.
If your cat is ill or has behavioural problems, please seek the advice of
a qualified professional, such as a vet or behavioural expert.

Contents

△ Eating sensibly
Make sure your cat's diet contains the correct balance of nutrients. Keep a check on his weight and adjust portion sizes if necessary.

▽ Sense of fun
Cats can be playful well into old age. There is plenty of scope for fun outdoors, but if you keep your cat indoors you need to provide him with entertainment.

△ Regular health checks
Help to keep your cat fit for life by monitoring his health with regular examinations at home and taking him to the vet for a routine annual check-up.

Introduction

It is not difficult to make room in your life for a cat. As millions of devoted owners have discovered, cats are good at adapting themselves to both small homes and large. They will settle happily for either being an exclusive companion in a one-person flat or claiming a share of attention in a busy family.

Cats are free spirits. Indoors or out, they like to suit themselves and go where they will – house rules permitting. They choose when to be sociable and when to stalk away. They do not want a daily walk, and most tolerate being left alone for long periods. But self-sufficient as these beautiful animals are, there is more to cat care than putting out bowls of food and providing a comfortable lap on demand. Cats depend on us to pay attention to their mental and physical health and welfare, and you will find useful advice here on how to interpret and respond to their behaviour.

The opening chapter will help you decide whether you are ready to take on the responsibility of cat ownership and offers guidance on essential equipment and the practicalities of making your home welcoming

▽ Feeling poorly
Cats don't complain when they are sick. It is up to us to recognize the signs of illness and take prompt action.

▽ Cat language
Your cat's behaviour can tell you many things – but you have to learn how to interpret his "language".

△ Wash and brush-up
Although cats are proficient at self-grooming, they need regular brushing and combing to keep their coats in peak condition. Shorthaired cats only need to be groomed once a week.

and cat-proof. This is followed by a wealth of advice on routine care – including grooming, bathing, and feeding at all stages of life from kitten to senior – as well as suggestions for coping with behavioural problems and, not least, having fun with your cat.

Two chapters on health explain the common cat disorders in detail, plus how to recognize the signs of ill-health, what to do for a sick cat or in an emergency situation and, most importantly, when to call in the vet. A final section discusses what is involved if you decide to breed from your cat and how to give the mother and her kittens the best possible care.

CONSULTANT
Alison L Logan, MA, VetMB, MRCVS, qualified in 1989 as a veterinary surgeon from the University of Cambridge, and has been in a small animal practice in her home town of Colchester ever since. She enjoys writing for lay and professional publications which have included *Cat World*, *Dogs Today*, *Veterinary Times*, *Veterinary Business Journal* and for *Pet Plan*. Alison has been overall winner of the Vetoquinol Literary Award twice, in 1995 and 2002. Alison wrote for a series of books on dog breeds, and was also a contributor to DK's *Complete Dog Care*.

1

Your new cat

Becoming a cat owner

Owning a cat can bring you and your family joy and companionship, but also many years of responsibility. Cats are active, intelligent, and long-lived, and they require continued care and attention.

First considerations

Before making the decision to buy or adopt a cat, think carefully about how he will fit into your lifestyle. Bear in mind, too, that your responsibilities may be long term – a cat can live for more than 20 years.

Could you give a cat daily attention? Most cats are relatively independent but some dislike being left alone all day. Never leave a cat unattended for more than 24 hours; in an emergency, make sure that someone is able to look in on him. If you regularly stay away from home, a cat may not be right for you.

Is a cat suitable for the whole family? A cat that was not raised with young children will likely find living with them stressful; and if

family members suffer from allergies or have restricted vision or mobility, a cat around the house is a potential hazard.

Do you want a kitten or an adult cat? Kittens need extra care and supervision, so be realistic about how much time you can allow for such things as litter-tray training and feeding up to four times a day. If you take on an adult cat, his previous experiences will influence how well he fits into your home. For example, a cat that is unused to children could find living with them stressful. (Rescue centres that rehome adult cats do their best to avoid such mismatches, see p.13.)

Will your cat live indoors or outdoors? Keeping a cat inside is generally safer but few homes can

provide all the stimulation that most cats require; adult cats that have always had access to the outside may not adapt well to an indoor lifestyle. Cats are hunters, so if your cat goes outside you must accept that he might bring home prey. In the house, a cat inevitably sheds hairs everywhere and may leave claw-marks on the furniture.

Would you prefer a quiet cat or a lively one? If you choose a pedigree (see pp.14–15), breed can indicate a cat's likely temperament, but a random-bred cat is more of an unknown quantity. In both cases, individual personality can be influenced by early life experiences and the parent cats' temperaments.

Do you want a male or female cat? Generally, neutered cats show no

> **"Cats** require a **surprising number** of resources… be sure you can afford **lifelong care."**

◁ **Starting young**
Kittens are usually more adaptable than older cats. If you acquire a kitten from a similar environment to your own home he is likely to settle in with little trouble.

◁ **Companionship**
Good cat care involves more than regular meals and a bed to sleep in. If your cat enjoys human company, it is essential to your cat's mental welfare to give him plenty of loving attention.

Owner responsibilities

■ Providing food and clean water
■ Meeting the cat's needs for companionship
■ Offering a choice of resources, such as beds and litter trays
■ Providing enough stimulation to ensure the cat stays fit and happy
■ Grooming (and bathing) when necessary
■ Socializing kittens so that they are confident in any situation
■ Seeking veterinary care when needed
■ Microchipping the cat and fitting him with a quick-release safety collar and ID tag

differences in behaviour and temperament. Unneutered toms may roam and spray urine, while on-heat females may be restless.

Essentials of cat care

Cats require a surprisingly large number of resources, and they can be expensive, so be sure that you can afford life-long care. Basic costs include buying food, bowls, beds, litter trays and/or a cat flap, a cat carrier, grooming equipment, veterinary care, microchipping, and insurance.

As well as providing for your cat's physical requirements, also consider his need for mental stimulation. Cats can quickly become bored, especially if they don't go outside regularly, and this can lead to destructive behaviours. There is a wide variety of cat toys and scratching posts available, but

taking time to interact with your cat is just as important as providing him with playthings. He will need plenty of stimulation in the form of cuddles and games.

Cats need regular grooming and the occasional bath. For a long-haired cat, daily grooming (see pp.32–3), taking up to half an hour, is essential. Shorthaired cats are

far less time-consuming but they need brushing or combing at least once a week.

From time to time you may have to arrange for cat care. This can incur considerable expense either for boarding fees if your pet stays in a cattery or for paying a professional cat-sitter.

You are morally, and in many countries also legally, responsible for your cat's welfare. Essential care includes giving your cat a safe home that enables him to perform normal cat behaviour, suitable food and clean water, preventive health care and veterinary treatment when necessary, and protection from unnecessary suffering.

◁ **Going away**
If your cat has to be left in someone else's care, he is still your responsibility. It may take time to find a reputable cattery or pet-sitting service that can provide the right level of attention.

Finding the right cat

Once you have decided that you are ready for the responsibility of being a cat owner, your search for the ideal pet begins. There are plenty of options, but you need to choose carefully to be sure of a happy outcome.

Where to look for a cat

Registered breeders are the most reliable people to approach if you are looking for a pedigree cat (see pp.14–15) For a non-pedigree cat, try rescue centres, your vet, or friends and neighbours that you know well. Be wary of buying a kitten or cat through a classified advertisement, especially one that also advertises a selection of other pets. The reality behind these offers may be animals that are reared in substandard conditions that leave them unprotected against diseases. For the same reason, it is best not to buy kittens from a pet shop. Although many pet shops are highly reputable, some may acquire their stock from dubious sources.

Visiting a breeder

Make an appointment with your chosen breeder to view a litter, and arrive armed with a list of points to look out for and questions to ask. If you are a first-time owner, do some homework in anticipation of the visit – both on the particular breed you have come to look at and on cat care in general. Good breeders want their kittens to go to responsible owners, so expect to have to answer questions as well as ask them.

You should be satisfied that the kittens are being kept in a clean, uncrowded, homely environment. It is also important to see them with their mother and siblings. Apart from being poor practice to

△ **Picking a pedigree**
Breeders sometimes have kittens ready for viewing, but you may have to wait until a litter is due and book ahead to make a visit.

remove young kittens from their family, you cannot judge their behaviour well if they are presented to you separately.

"Do not allow yourself to **fall for a kitten** simply because it looks in need of **extra love."**

It should be obvious whether or not the kittens have been well socialized and are used to being handled. This would have been achieved by speaking to, playing with, and holding them from a young age. If a breeder has neglected this side of their welfare

◁ **Family group**
Always ask to see young kittens together with their mother and siblings. They should not be removed from their family and shown to you separately.

you will find it difficult, if not impossible, to make up for lost time once you get your kitten home.

Your chosen kitten should appear alert and active, with a healthy coat, bright eyes with no signs of discharge, and clean ears. Do not allow yourself to fall for a kitten simply because it looks in need of extra love. A kitten that is lagging behind its siblings may have health problems. Ask if the kitten has been screened for any genetic disorders common to the breed, and check that it has been vaccinated and wormed, or that it will have been by the time you take it home. Also enquire if the breeder is prepared to provide any after-purchase support or will take back the kitten should serious defects or problems arise.

Pedigrees are expensive, but breeders sometimes offer kittens at a lower price because they are not "show quality". However, even without symmetrical markings or perfect conformation (breed characteristics), these usually make beautiful and lovable pets.

Cat shelters

Cat shelters, or rescue centres, are packed with kittens and adult cats of all types and ages in need of rehousing. Most of the cats offered for adoption are random bred, but the occasional pedigree can be found too. Not all rescue cats have been abandoned or ill-treated and have subsequent behavioural problems: sometimes a previous owner had to part with a pet because of personal circumstances,

such as a bereavement or a relocation abroad, and a cat that has already had one loving home is likely to settle well into another.

The first step towards adoption is a home visit from a member of the shelter's staff (see box below). Once the shelter introduces you to some cats, they will tell you as much as possible about each cat's background and personality, and whether there are any health issues to consider. They can also give advice on cat care, including neutering, and offer back-up support following an adoption.

All cats taken into shelters are routinely given a health check, vaccinated, and treated for fleas

and internal parasites. If an adoption is agreed, you will be asked to pay a fee to help cover these expenses.

Adopting a stray

Some people are chosen by their cat. A stray that hangs around can easily work its way into family affections, but before offering your visitor a permanent home, make sure that it really is a stray: many cats lead double lives. Make every effort to trace a possible owner by looking for local "cat missing" notices, posting up notices yourself, speaking to neighbours, or asking a vet to check whether the cat is microchipped (see p.89).

Having an assessment

Adopting a cat from a shelter is a two-way process. You not only hope to find the "right" cat, but you have to be right for him, too. The centre will assess your potential as a cat owner by asking questions about your circumstances and commitment to cat care, and will arrange a home visit to see what type of environment you can provide. For example, if you live in a flat or do not have a garden, a cat accustomed to a free-roving outdoor life may not be ideal. Some cats may not be suited to living with children. Your lifestyle will also need to be taken into account: it may not be possible for you to adopt a kitten if you will be out of the house at work all day.

Choosing a cat breed

There is a bewildering variety of shapes and sizes, colours, and coat types to choose from if you opt for a pedigree cat. However much looks appeal, you should consider a breed's personality and needs before coming to a decision.

Do your research

Most people fall in love with a particular breed of cat because of its looks, but there are other important points to consider. Different breeds have distinct characteristics and varying requirements in terms of daily care, companionship, space to roam, and mental stimulation. You cannot have a happy cat if your lifestyle is not compatible with the breed's temperament. And you will not be a happy owner if your pet is a noisy and hyperactive mischief-maker when you wanted a peaceable lap cat.

The advantage of having a pedigree cat is that you can find out beforehand what you could be letting yourself in for. Do some research in advance – breed websites are often an excellent source of information. If possible, visit a cat show on a fact-finding mission, but be prepared to find all the breeds you look at equally appealing.

▷ **Maine Coon**
One of the largest of all cat breeds, the Maine Coon is a gentle giant with a playful nature. The shaggy, semi-longhaired coat changes seasonally; be prepared for heavy shedding of the thick undercoat in warmer weather.

△ **Persian**
Sweet-tempered and home-loving, a Persian likes to take life quietly. Daily grooming is essential to prevent the long coat from tangling or matting. The Golden Persian shown here is just one of the many colour variations available.

◁ **Exotic Shorthair**
A shorter-coated version of the Persian, the Exotic has the same round-faced appeal and placid temperament of its cousin, but needs far less grooming. Content to spend life indoors, it makes a good pet for flat-dwellers.

△ **Siamese**
There is never a dull moment with a Siamese in the house. Noisy, mischievous, and always on the go, this cat expects a lot of attention, which it repays with devoted attachment to its owner.

▷ **Russian Blue**
This lithe and leggy breed with a smoky, plush coat has become extremely popular over the last century. Russian Blues are calm, easy to live with, and very affectionate towards their owner, although a little reserved with strangers.

Bengal
Originally developed by crossing domestic cats with the wild Asian leopard cat, the dramatically patterned Bengal is a rare breed. It has no "wild" traits, but possesses boundless energy and is unhappy without constant amusement and companionship.

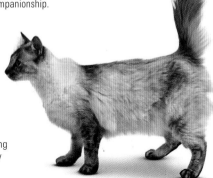

▷ Balinese
With a dancer's grace and a silky coat, this longhaired version of the Siamese is exquisitely beautiful. The Balinese is an all-action cat that does not appreciate being left to entertain itself for any length of time.

◁ Sphynx
Hairless cats are not everyone's choice, but the elfish Sphynx's endearing character has won the breed a solid fan base. Sphynxes should be kept indoors and protected from extreme temperatures. The skin needs regular washing to remove excess body oils.

△ Burmese
Being with the family means a lot to a Burmese – this is not a cat to leave at home alone all day. It is intelligent and inquisitive, and makes a loyal and loving companion.

◁ British Shorthair
Considered by many to be the perfect household cat, the British Shorthair is handsome, robust, and adaptable to either a town or country lifestyle. It likes comfort and company but does not pester for attention.

△ Abyssinian
Not a cat to laze on the sofa, the Abyssinian needs plenty of scope for play and exploration, and would best suit an experienced owner. It has a striking appearance with a strong, elegant body and beautiful ticked fur.

▷ Cornish Rex
This breed's defining feature is its tightly waved coat. The Cornish Rex is an athlete and an acrobat, and thrives on fun. Because its fur is fine, the cat is sensitive to heat and cold and needs very gentle grooming.

Making your home safe

It is feline nature to want to get into and onto everything, and making a house or garden completely cat-proof would be impossible. However, you can reduce the likelihood of mishaps with a few basic precautions.

Free to roam?

If you have a choice, should you let your cat go in and out as he pleases? Undoubtedly, there are greater risks outdoors – especially from traffic, territorial fights, and cat thieves. On the other hand, confining an inquisitive cat indoors can lead to havoc in the house. Take your pet's personality into account when deciding on the limits of his freedom.

◁ **Night prowler**
You may worry about your pet's safety if he stays out after dark. Some owners let their cats roam outside in daytime but prefer to keep them in at night.

Hazards in the home

Most potential dangers are found in the kitchen. Never leave anything unattended that your cat could jump on or knock over, such as a switched-on hotplate, an iron, a boiling saucepan, or sharp utensils. Keep the doors of washing machines or tumble dryers closed, but first make sure your cat is not inside.

Cats are less inclined than dogs to steal food, raid the rubbish bin, or chew up forbidden items, but they still need protecting from substances that could make them ill. Keep them away from wet paint and chemical cleaners, which are easily transferred from walls and floors to fur, and then licked off and swallowed. Check that there are no dangers lurking in the carpet, such as drawing pins, needles, or shards of broken glass or china.

Outdoor checklist

■ Shut shed and garage doors to prevent access to chemicals or sharp tools
■ Cover fishponds with netting to stop kittens falling in or older cats poaching fish; empty out paddling pools when not in use
■ Place bird feeders out of reach
■ Prevent your cat from touching rodent bait or poisoned animals
■ Cover your children's sandpit to prevent use as a litter tray
■ Keep your cat indoors if you have fireworks or a bonfire

DO...
consider planting a tree for shade and for use as a scratching post.

DO...
watch neighbouring cats for signs of aggression.

DO...
shut away garden chemicals and tools, but before locking up a shed check that your cat is not inside.

◁ **Watching the world**
A window ledge is a good place to just sit and stare. If the window is on an upper floor, make sure your cat cannot jump out.

Close off exit points above ground floor level. Cats can climb out of upper-floor windows, or over a high-rise balcony, with serious consequences.

Hazards in the garden

While cats rarely nibble anything but grass, it is wise to check your garden for toxic plants. Ponds and paddling pools are possible hazards, especially for kittens. Until a kitten knows his way around, take him out in a harness on a lead. Chemicals

and tools should be shut away in a shed or garage – make sure you do not accidently shut your cat in too. The major concern for owners is the road outside. High fencing is expensive, but could deter your cat from wandering and also keep other cats out.

Do not forget to protect your garden against the cat. Children's sandpits and soft earth make inviting litter trays, so cover the sand when not in use and scatter cat deterrents around precious plants.

Indoor checklist

■ Never leave heated kitchen appliances, such as cookers and irons, unattended

■ Do not leave sharp utensils and breakables within the cat's reach

■ Shut the doors of cupboards and appliances such as washing machines and tumble dryers

■ Keep your cat away from wet paint or surfaces wet with cleaning chemicals

■ Protect open fires with a guard

■ Ensure that your cat cannot jump out of upper floor windows

■ Do not place toxic houseplants where your cat could brush against them

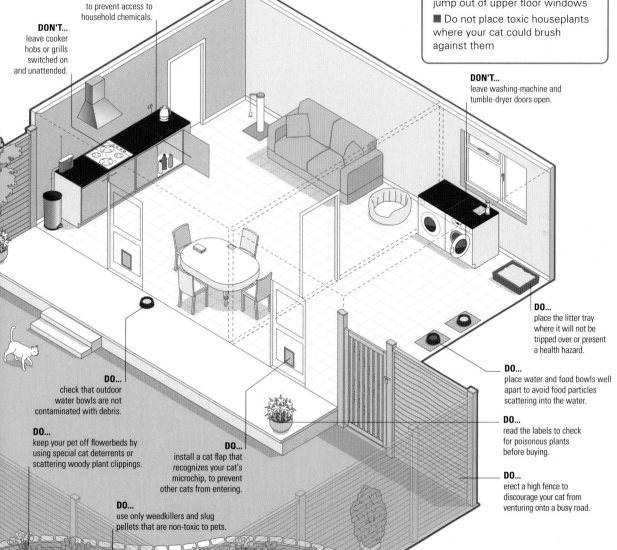

DO... secure cupboard doors to prevent access to household chemicals.

DON'T... leave cooker hobs or grills switched on and unattended.

DON'T... leave washing-machine and tumble-dryer doors open.

DO... place the litter tray where it will not be tripped over or present a health hazard.

DO... place water and food bowls well apart to avoid food particles scattering into the water.

DO... read the labels to check for poisonous plants before buying.

DO... erect a high fence to discourage your cat from venturing onto a busy road.

DO... check that outdoor water bowls are not contaminated with debris.

DO... keep your pet off flowerbeds by using special cat deterrents or scattering woody plant clippings.

DO... install a cat flap that recognizes your cat's microchip, to prevent other cats from entering.

DO... use only weedkillers and slug pellets that are non-toxic to pets.

Essential equipment

There are a few essentials that should be in place before a new cat arrives. Once you get to know your pet's preferences and personality, you can choose more particular items and equipment.

Comfort first

Cats are good at making themselves comfortable and have an unerring eye for the best places to curl up in and snooze. They are more than willing to share your favourite armchair or cushions, or the duvet on your bed, if that is permitted. Most people delight in seeing their cat make free use of the home – and will be prepared to forgive the nest made in a pile of newly laundered towels. However, cats do need a safe and special bed that is indisputably their own.

There is a wide range of cat beds on the market, from baskets and roofed-in tent-style beds to bean bags and hammocks. From an owner's point of view, whether the bed looks attractive and is easy to wash may be priorities. From your cat's point of view, soft fabrics that generate warmth – such as

△ **Cats like high places**
A hammock bed hung from a radiator or mounted on the wall provides both a cosy retreat and a good vantage point.

fleece – are desirable, as are beds with soft sides to snuggle up against. You can always add a folded blanket or a cushion for extra padding. Do not buy your cat the equivalent of a king-sized bed under the impression that he will enjoy stretching out in it. Cats usually prefer to sleep somewhere fairly compact that gives them a sense of wrap-around security.

Food and water bowls

Your cat needs separate bowls for food and water, and if you have more than one cat each should have his own set. Bowls can be either plastic or metal and should have a wide base that prevents them from being tipped over. Buy bowls that are shallow-sided and fairly wide – cats do not like having their whiskers cramped while they are eating or drinking. If you are out of the house for long periods, it may be worth buying an automatic feeder. Such feeders have a lid to prevent the food from going stale and are set with a timer to pop open at your cat's regular mealtime (see pp.26–7 and pp.28–9).

Cat carriers

Even if you borrow a carrier just to bring a new cat home in, it is wise to invest in one of your own. There

Litter trays

A cat likes a litter tray to himself, so more than one cat means more than one tray. Litter trays should be fairly large with sides high enough to prevent spillages when the cat scrapes the litter around. Litter materials made of clay or absorbent pellets are the most convenient to use, as they form clumps when wet, which are easy to scoop up.

Scoop
Fibre pellets
Clay pellets
Litter tray

Plastic bowl

Steel bowl
△ **Choosing bowls**
Choose wide-based food and water bowls that are sturdy enough not to slide around the floor when your cat uses them.

△ **Basket-style bed**
Soft fabric beds with high sides are nearly as good as the sofa for snuggling into. Check that the material is easy to wash.

△ **Tent-style bed**
This type of bed, sometimes referred to as an "igloo", keeps out draughts and gives your cat the security of a roof over his head.

Collars and ID tags

If your cat ventures outdoors, it makes sense for him to wear a collar carrying an address tag in case he gets lost (see also "Microchipping" on p.89). However, collars tend to snag on branches or undergrowth. To avoid the risk of a cat being caught up and possibly choked, fit a collar with a quick-release fastener that snaps open when tugged. Collars with elastic inserts are unsafe, because some may stretch enough to become stuck around the head or allow the cat to put a leg through.

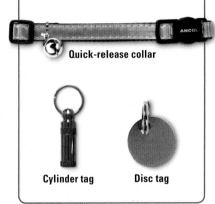

Quick-release collar

Cylinder tag   **Disc tag**

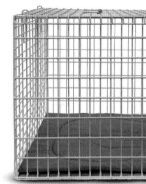

△ **Carrier**
A carrier made of rigid plastic is easy to clean and resistant to a cat's scratching. It protects the cat against knocks and bumps during travel.

△ **Wire travelling cage**
Your cat may travel better if he can see out all the way round. Cages usually open from the top and some fold flat for storage.

are bound to be times when you will need to transport your cat safely for trips to the vet, or maybe to a cattery when you go on holiday. If your cat gets used to the look and smell of his carrier, he is less likely to be stressed when a journey becomes necessary. Let him climb in and out of it at home, and he will soon regard it as part of his personal territory.

Cat carriers are made of various materials, including basketwork, rigid plastic, coated wire, and soft fabrics. Most cats object to being confined, so it is important to choose a carrier with a wide grid opening that lets your cat see out and allows you to communicate

with him. Many carriers are made in two halves, so that the top half can be unclipped and taken off and your pet easily lifted in and out. Make sure that the carrier gives your cat enough room to turn around. Line the bottom with one of his old blankets to provide a familiar smell. Soft-sided carriers, in the style of tote bags, are the easiest to carry and most comfortable for your cat. However, they can be tricky to clean and may provide less ventilation than rigid carriers. The most economical option is a cardboard carrier, but this type may not withstand assault from a cat determined to claw his way out

and is best used as a temporary measure for short journeys.

Something to play with

Ready-made cat toys perhaps cannot be counted as essential equipment, but most owners find them impossible to resist. They are an amusing way of keeping an indoor pet physically and mentally fit. Cats have a natural sense of fun and even mature, sedentary cats can be persuaded to play for a few moments. Swiping at a feather on a wire or ripping up a catnip mouse is good exercise – although your cat will be just as happy with scrumpled newspaper or a cardboard box (see pp.38–9).

Bringing your cat home

Getting a new pet is a big event and all concerned are bound to feel a little anxious and excited. Plan ahead and stay calm – most cats settle in very quickly and soon act as if they own the place.

Ready and waiting

Before welcoming home your new cat, have everything for his safety and comfort organized in advance. Check for obvious hazards in both the house and garden (see pp.16–17), and choose an inviting corner for his bed and feed bowls. Stock up enough cat food to last for several days – buy several different varieties so that you can find out which appeals to him the most.

Decide on a place for a litter tray that will provide privacy for the cat and cause no inconvenience or hygiene problems for you. If you are getting a kitten, having a stack of newspaper ready for accidents is always useful.

Arrival day

When your kitten or cat arrives, he will probably be nervous and stressed after being confined for the journey. Place the carrier in a quiet room where he can see familiar-looking objects, such as a bowl of food. Some cats will step forward boldly the moment the carrier is opened, while others hang back. Do not force a shy cat out of his carrier. Call him gently, using the name you have chosen, and let him absorb the new sights and smells. Do not hover too closely; just watch for that tentative paw to appear.

Let your new cat explore places he is allowed to go. On the first day, it may help to build his confidence if you keep him to just one room with everything he needs readily accessible.

△ **Stepping into a new home**
Do not lift your cat out of his carrier the moment you get him home, however excited you are. Just talk to him quietly and let him emerge in his own time.

For the next few weeks, or at least until the cat has learned to respond to his name, it is safest to make the garden out of bounds. A young kitten should not be allowed outside until he has been fully vaccinated – usually by the time he is 13–14 weeks old.

Meeting the family

When a cat or kitten is introduced to a family and other pets, it takes a while for everyone to feel comfortable. Explain to children before you bring the cat home that an animal is not an exciting toy for

△ **Going exploring**
It's all new and strange, but your cat will soon start exploring and getting accustomed to his surroundings. Before long, he will have chosen a few favourite corners.

◁ **Handle with care**
Show children how to stroke their pet gently and calmly. Explain that cats should not be picked up unnecessarily or overwhelmed with attention.

of introductions to the newcomer and should definitely not run loose in the same room as an adult cat. Feline hunting instincts are very close to the surface.

Establishing a routine

Setting up a regular routine right from the start will help your cat to feel secure. Establish feeding times and use these as an opportunity to teach your cat to come when called. Kittens may not know how to use a litter tray (see pp.86–7) and, in the strangeness of a new home, even an adult cat can have accidents. Place your kitten or cat on his tray at regular intervals, such as after a meal, until using the litter tray is second nature. To avoid problems later on, stick to the rules about no-go areas for your cat – for example, do not allow him to sleep on the bed "just this once".

them to play with. Scratches, tears, and a terrified cat make the worst possible start, so supervise children if necessary while they are getting to know their pet. Discourage loud voices and boisterous games, and step in at once to prevent inappropriate handling.

An older cat already in the household will almost certainly take a dim view of a stranger encroaching on his personal territory. Never place litter trays or food bowls side by side and expect the resident and the newcomer to sort it out for themselves. Keep the cats apart to begin with, but allow them to become accustomed to each other's scent, either by swapping over feeding bowls (so that they also associate the scent with the pleasure of food), or by moving them into each other's rooms. After a week or so, introduce them but do not leave them alone together.

Make sure that neither cat feels trapped but has somewhere to run to if tempers become frayed. After a few such meetings, the chances are that the cats will tolerate one another, even if they never become best friends. Resident cats seem to be less likely to show aggression towards a young kitten than to another adult cat.

Introductions between cats and dogs are not necessarily the problem you might expect. Although much depends on the breed, not all dogs are inveterate cat chasers. For the first few meetings, keep the dog on a lead and leave the cat space to back off. Talk to both animals softly, give them equal attention, and praise your dog if he behaves well. Never leave the two alone together until you are confident that the relationship is going to be peaceful.

Small pets, such as hamsters or rabbits, are probably best left out

△ **Using the litter tray**
Cats need a little time to get used to a new litter tray in an unfamiliar position. They dislike being on view, so place the tray in a discreet corner.

Understanding your cat

Cats did not evolve to be social animals. Highly independent, they have developed subtle and complex ways of behaving and communicating that often send confusing messages to their owners.

Cat behaviour

Domestic cats evolved from a small, solitary, and territorial predator that rarely met others of its kind. This feline ancestor did not need to develop a complex visual communication system like that of more naturally social species, such as dogs and humans, so our pet cats today do not have a particularly sophisticated body language. Their solitary past also means that cats are more independent than most other pet species and although many enjoy cuddles, they still appreciate their own space.

Cats are supreme hunters and as their prey is more active at dawn and dusk this is when cats are most active. Motivation to hunt at these times might cause your cat to have a "mad half-hour", where he dashes about energetically.

Because their eyesight evolved primarily to detect movement in poor light, cats do not see patterns or colours with the same clarity as humans do. Their eyes are not sensitive to colours at the red end of the spectrum and, as a result, they may have difficulty in picking out red toys against a pink carpet. On the other hand, they are extremely quick to respond to a trailing string.

The sense of smell is very important to cats. They head-rub to deposit scent in areas where they

△ **Scent marking**
Cats identify each other by smell and create a group identity by rubbing against each other to deposit scent. They often also rub their owners to make them part of the social group.

◁ **Solitary nature**
Domestic cats have retained much of the solitary and independent nature of their ancestors. This means that when two cats cross paths there is often conflict.

◁ **Getting on well**
Other cats can often be seen as competition and a threat to survival. To reduce stress in the house, introduce cats carefully and provide them with separate resources.

When conflict arises, cats cannot use body language to defuse the situation. This is why fights can break out just as easily between members of the same household as between rivals from opposite sides of the garden fence.

Handling your cat

Cats rarely enjoy being picked up – watch out for lip licking – so only lift your cat when necessary, unless you are sure he enjoys it. Handle him calmly and quietly, stroking his head, back, and cheeks to relax him. If he rubs or noses your hand you know that he is enjoying the attention. Never lift your cat by the scruff but pick up him gently by supporting his chest, behind the front legs, and hindquarters at the same time. Hold him upright, as cradling in your arms can increase his sense of insecurity.

feel relaxed and spray urine where they feel threatened. Cats also use scent to orientate themselves in their environment, following "scent maps" created from scent glands in the feet and flanks. Any upheaval in the home – such as redecorating or moving house – can disrupt this mapping system, causing a cat to feel displaced and bewildered.

Although a cat's body language is quite subtle, it is important to learn to recognize when your pet does

forward, he is licking his lips and his weight is shifted onto his back feet then you should leave him alone as these are signs of fear.

Cats in company

Cats can happily live together in social groups, but only under specific circumstances. Groups largely consist of related females that hunt independently and do not compete for food and territory. They show friendly behaviours to

"Although **many cats enjoy cuddles**, they still **appreciate** their **own space.**"

and does not want attention. A cat will greet you by approaching with his tail up, and may rub against your legs. Rubbing deposits scent, making you smell more familiar after you have been outside or in the shower. Purring and kneading with the paws in response to owner attention are behaviours retained from kittenhood, when they were associated with suckling. Although purring usually indicates contentment it can sometimes indicate pain. When a cat's ears are flattened, his whiskers bunched

each other, reserving aggression for "outsiders" that represent a threat to resources. Even though their owners provide food, cats will still protect their territory from others that are not part of their social group. If you have more than one cat, watch them to determine whether they are friends or not. Friends rub and groom each other and sleep together with bodies touching. If you do not see at least one of these behaviours then it is likely that your cats feel stressed by each other.

△ **The tactful touch**
Although most cats enjoy some attention, many of them feel uncomfortable or nervous if they are picked up. If your pet objects to being held, put him down before he becomes stressed.

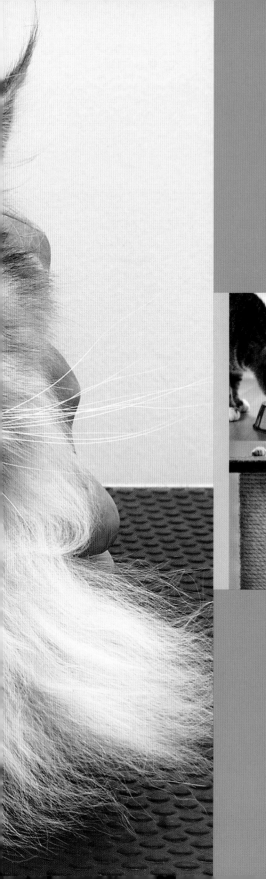

2

Everyday care

A **balanced diet**

To stay healthy, cats need a regular intake of certain nutrients. You should provide your pet with a diet that not only satisfies hunger but also provides all the essential food elements.

The right nutrients

Meat is the natural diet for cats. A feline digestive system is not designed to process large amounts of vegetable matter, although it is usual for cats to chew a little grass now and then. Regardless of your own food preferences, you cannot turn your cat into a vegetarian without putting his health, and even his life, at risk.

Prey caught in the wild supplies not just meat protein but also essential fats, vitamins, minerals – such as calcium from bones – and fibre. Domestic cats are unlikely to have to hunt for their meals, and they are not natural scavengers, so they rely on us to supply the correct nutrients, whether in ready-made or home-cooked food. Cats are notoriously picky eaters, so you may have to experiment with foods of different types, textures, and flavours before you hit on the ones that bring your pet hurrying to his feed bowl.

Ready-prepared foods

Supermarket shelves offer a huge selection of prepared cat foods in almost every gourmet flavour imaginable. So which ones should you choose?

Most commercial cat foods are complete foods, that is, they provide all necessary nutrients and do not need anything else added. However, some products may be labelled "complementary", in which case they need to be combined with other foods to provide balanced nutrition. Check the information on the package to be sure which type you are buying.

Dry food, which comes in the form of small pellets or biscuits, can be left in the bowl for a cat to

△ **Natural fibre**
Cats need fibre in their diet, which should be supplied by correct feeding. In the wild, a cat will obtain nutrients from prey.

◁ **A healthy appetite**
Your cat knows what he likes, but it is important that his favourite foods contain the right balance of nutrients to maintain good health.

Dry food

Wet food

Home-cooked food

nibble at throughout the day – a great advantage for owners who cannot always be home at regular times. Some owners feed their cat exclusively on dry food, but it is better to provide a little variety by offering the occasional meal of wet food instead. Dry food gives a cat something to chew on and helps to keep teeth and gums in good condition.

Moist or "wet" food, which comes in tins or sealed pouches, looks appetizing and is usually enjoyed by the majority of cats. Moist food keeps well until opened, but any left uneaten in a feed bowl should be thrown away. This could prove expensive if your pet is a fussy eater and rejects one flavour after another.

Fresh food

If you prefer to give your cat home-cooked food – and avoid the preservatives found in commercial products – you should apply the same standards for buying and preparing it as you would for your own meals. However, great care is needed to provide a balanced diet because your cat has highly specialized dietary requirements and could quickly run into health problems if his diet is deficient in, for example, taurine. Whether you use red meat, chicken, or fish, obtain it from a reputable source and cook it thoroughly to destroy

△ **Dry, wet, and home-cooked food**
Offer your cat a variety of ready-prepared and home-cooked foods to keep him interested in his meals. Make sure all his dietary needs are met.

any disease-causing organisms. Cut meat into pieces that your cat can eat easily, and remove any bones. If you are not confident that home-cooked food will provide your cat with the right level of nutrition, ask your vet for a diet sheet.

Titbits and supplements

Offering a titbit now and then does no harm, but if you hand out treats too often you may find that your cat is piling on extra weight. Commercially made cat treats, which are nutritionally balanced, are preferable to possibly unhealthy scraps from the table (see box, right).

A healthy cat on a well-rounded diet should not need additional vitamins and minerals. Dosing your cat with supplements without veterinary advice is not a good idea, and may even cause illness.

Water

Your cat needs constant access to clean water, both indoors and outdoors, especially if he eats mostly dry food. Keep water bowls well apart from feeding bowls to avoid contamination from scattered food, change the water frequently, and remember in particular to check that water bowls left in the garden are not full of debris.

△ **Clean water**
Provide fresh water in both house and garden so that your cat can drink any time he wants. Keep the water bowls scrupulously clean.

Harmful foods

■ Milk and cream can cause diarrhoea, as most cats do not have the necessary enzymes to digest dairy products. Special-formula "cat milk" is available

■ Onions, garlic, and chives cause gastric upsets and may lead to anaemia

■ Grapes and raisins are thought to cause kidney damage

■ The alkaloid theobromine in chocolate is highly toxic to cats

■ Raw eggs may contain the bacteria that cause food poisoning. Uncooked egg white disrupts vitamin B absorption in cats, leading to skin problems

■ Raw meat and fish may contain harmful enzymes and also cause fatal bacterial poisoning

■ Small splintery bones in cooked food can become lodged in the throat or further down the digestive tract, causing blockage and tearing the intestinal lining

Monitoring feeding levels

From kittenhood to the senior years, nutritional requirements for cats vary as their rates of growth and activity levels alter. By adjusting a cat's diet to suit age and lifestyle, you can keep your pet at a healthy weight.

Good feeding habits

Establishing a regular feeding routine helps you to control the amount of food your cat eats and allows you to spot any changes in his appetite. Good hygiene is just as important as the food that is provided. Make a few simple rules and stick to them:

■ Feed at regular times, if possible.

■ Restrict treats to a minimum.

■ Never offer titbits from your own meals.

■ Offer new flavours and textures occasionally to prevent boredom with food.

■ If you need to make changes to your cat's diet, introduce them gradually.

■ Throw away leftovers in the bowl before food goes stale or attracts flies.

■ Keep food and water bowls scrupulously clean.

Maintaining an ideal weight

By checking your cat's weight and girth regularly, you will soon recognize if he is getting fat or becoming too thin (see box, opposite). If you have any concerns, take your cat to the vet to be weighed.

It is hard to refuse a cat who appears to be ready for a second helping, but overfeeding soon leads to obesity. Being overweight is just as unhealthy for cats as it is for humans. Appetite is not necessarily linked to a high-energy lifestyle; many inactive cats are capable of packing away enormous meals. Indoor cats have the highest risk of obesity – some types are naturally sedentary and need encouraging to climb down from the sofa now and then. Outdoor cats are more likely to burn up the energy they get from food.

Packaged foods give some guidelines on how much to feed, but the amounts suggested are only approximate. If your pet is becoming rotund, even though you are careful with portion sizes, suspect him of cadging meals elsewhere. A conversation with the neighbours may solve the mystery.

Feeding a cat
It is good to see your cat showing enthusiasm for meals, but it can be hard to distinguish hunger from greed. Some inactive cats pester for food out of boredom.

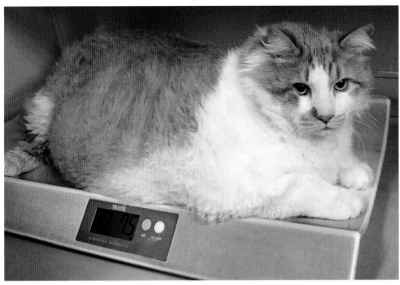

◁ **Weight-watching**
Almost overflowing the veterinary scales, this overindulged cat could be heading for serious health problems unless his weight is reduced by adjustments to his diet.

"It is **hard to refuse** a cat who appears to be ready for a **second helping**, but overfeeding soon leads to **obesity.**"

Weight loss without a change in diet should never be ignored, as it can be an early warning sign of illness. Very elderly cats do tend to become thinner with age, but you should ensure that there are no underlying problems such as loose teeth. Have your cat checked by the vet if he is refusing food or has difficulty chewing.

Dietary changes throughout life

Cats have different nutritional needs at different times of life in terms of both type and quantity of food. Kittens need a high-protein diet to sustain their rapid development. There are many commercial brands of food specially formulated for them. In their first few months, kittens should be fed smaller amounts at more frequent intervals than adult cats; four to six tiny meals a day would be the average for a kitten that has just started on solids. Later, you can increase the portions and reduce the number of meals.

Most adult cats in good health do well on two meals a day. Even the most hyperactive adult should never be fed on high-protein kitten food, which can lead to kidney malfunction. As a cat ages, his appetite often diminishes and you may need to revert to feeding him little and often again. The commercial cat food market caters for seniors just as it does for kittens.

If cats need special diets, such as during pregnancy and when nursing kittens, or to control weight or a medical condition, a vet's advice is essential. Introduce any new feeding regime in easy stages, as a rapid change can cause digestive upsets.

Assessing condition

You cannot always judge by appearance alone whether a cat is too fat or too thin, especially if he is longhaired. Learn to assess his weight by the feel of his body, gently running your hands around his back, ribs, and belly.

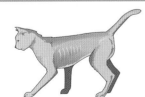

△ **Underweight**
There is little or no fat over the ribs, spine, and hip bones. The cat's belly is "tucked up", and there is a noticeable hollow behind the ribcage.

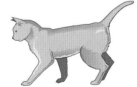

△ **Ideal weight**
The ribs can be felt through a thin layer of fat, and there is a slight narrowing of the body behind the ribcage. The belly has only a small covering of fat.

△ **Overweight**
The ribs and spine cannot be felt through a thick layer of fat. Heavy pads of fat cover the belly and there is no discernible "waistline" behind the ribcage.

Regular grooming

Although staying well-groomed comes naturally to cats, by assisting with regular grooming sessions, you can enjoy a bonding experience and help your pet to look good. A clean coat is healthy and comfortable.

Benefits of grooming

Cats spend a large part of the day self-grooming – wetting their paws to wipe their face, cleaning between each toe, and twisting their flexible spine to reach awkward places such as shoulders and anal areas. The surface of a cat's tongue is covered with minute barbs and these act as a comb to collect skin debris and loose hairs and to smooth out tangles. In fact, cats are so particular about daily grooming that it may not seem necessary to give them any extra help.

One reason for grooming your cat is that it strengthens the bond between you and your pet. Grooming cats from a young age helps to establish this special bond. Most cats enjoy the close contact with their owners and

△ **Reaching the corners**
Cats are clean animals and spend hours industriously washing themselves. They usually start at the head before attending to each area of the body.

the sensation of being brushed or combed. You can also give your cat a general check-up while grooming. Take the opportunity to inspect eyes, ears, and claws, and

to monitor your cat for possible health problems such as parasites, hidden injuries, lumps and bumps, and changes in weight.

Another benefit is that regular grooming helps to reduce the amount of loose hairs that cats lick up and swallow. Normally, the hair forms into harmless balls in the stomach, which the cat then coughs up. However, sometimes the balls become large enough to be a health hazard, causing choking or becoming lodged in the lower gut, and causing a blockage.

In old age, cats sometimes lose their enthusiasm for hygiene and may need gentle grooming to help them maintain dignity and cleanliness. The sudden neglect of self-grooming in cats of any age is a warning sign that all is not well, and needs to be investigated by a vet.

Coat types

In longhaired cats such as Persians, the undercoat can be massively thick. The coat not only collects debris from around the home and garden but tends to form tangles that no amount of licking can remove. Neglected tangles can easily turn into impenetrable mats, especially in areas of the body where there is friction, such as the armpits.

◁ **Moulting season**
A slicker brush with wire pins is an excellent tool for removing loose hairs, especially when a cat is shedding a thick undercoat in warmer weather.

△ Longhaired
Persians and other types of longhaired cats need daily grooming to prevent the fur from tangling and matting. The thick undercoat sheds heavily.

△ Semi-longhaired
With a silky topcoat and a lighter undercoat than longhairs, these cats are unlikely to develop tangles and are generally easy to groom.

△ Wavy or curly
Coats of this type vary in length. All versions can be spoiled by over-grooming, so bathing is preferable. Shedding is usually light.

△ Shorthaired
Easy-care shorthairs largely look after themselves, but weekly grooming serves both as a bonding session and an opportunity for a health check.

△ Hairless
Unabsorbed body oils build up in hairless cats and can sometimes lead to skin problems. Regular wiping or bathing is necessary for these cats.

Even the most fastidious longhaired cats simply cannot keep their coats in good order by their own efforts, so owners need to lend a hand. In extreme cases there will be no option but to cut the matted hair away – a task that needs professional skill. Longhairs are also at greater risk than shorthairs of collecting large furballs. If you own a longhaired cat, a daily grooming session is necessary (see pp.32–3).

Semi-longhaired cats, which include Maine Coons and the Balinese, have a silky topcoat and a minimal undercoat, so their fur remains free from matting and tangling. Weekly brushing and combing is all that is required.

Some cats have fine, wavy, or rippled coats, as seen in the Cornish Rex, and a few breeds sport longer curls. Such coats do not shed heavily and are not as difficult to maintain as might be imagined. Over-vigorous grooming can spoil the appearance of the fur, so bathing rather than brushing is often recommended for this type of cat (see pp.34–5).

Shorthaired cats have a topcoat of sleek guard hairs and a soft, downy undercoat of varying thickness. Although the undercoat may shed quite heavily, especially in warm weather, these cats are generally very easy to maintain. Grooming once a week is usually sufficient for shorthairs.

Hairless cats such as the Sphynx are not usually entirely bald but have an overlay of fine fuzz. This thin covering is not enough to absorb the natural body oils that are secreted through the skin and regular bathing is needed to prevent a greasy build-up.

Grooming tools

Buy tools intended specifically for cats, and keep a separate set for each cat in the family. Basic items include a wide-toothed comb or a bristle brush for removing tangles, and a slicker brush, which has wire pins set in a rubber base. The slicker is invaluable for sweeping up loosened hairs and debris from the coat. If your cat lives indoors and cannot keep his claws trim by scratching, you may need a pair of sharp clippers to remove the claw tips (ask a professional to show you how to do this). A tick remover is useful for outdoor cats living in country areas.

Fine comb

Tick remover

Slicker brush

Nail clippers

Soft-bristled brush

Step-by-step grooming

Whether you groom your cat daily or weekly, aim to make every session enjoyable, and not too stressful for either of you. Use the grooming tools correctly and give your cat confidence by being calm and methodical.

To put your cat in a relaxed mood for grooming, spend a few moments making a quiet fuss of him before you start. Grooming a longhair thoroughly can take up to half an hour, but if you make it a daily routine there will be fewer time-consuming tangles to deal with. Never try to pin down a protesting cat that has had enough for one session. Release him if he starts to object, give him a treat, and have another go later.

"Spend a **few moments** making a **quiet fuss** of him **before you start.**"

1. ▽

Combing through
Begin by gently combing the cat from head to tail with a wide-toothed comb, following the natural lie of the fur. Do not tug at knots or tangles – tease them out carefully with your fingers.

2. ▷

Removing debris
Use a slicker brush with fine pins or a soft-bristle brush to collect loosened hairs and skin debris from both the undercoat and topcoat. This helps to make the fur look full and shiny.

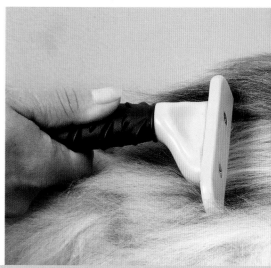

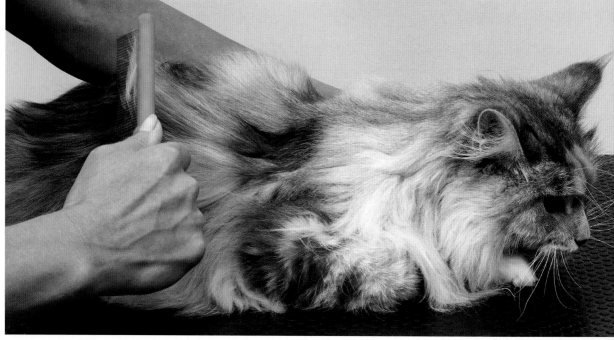

3 ◁
Trimming mats
Badly matted fur may need removing with clippers. Leave this job to a professional, as unskilled attempts could result in injury to the cat's skin.

4 △
Finishing touches
To end the session, fluff up the coat with a wide-toothed comb to make it stand out and comb through long plumes on the tail.

Grooming the face

Clean your cat's face each time you groom him, and use the opportunity to check for problems such as runny eyes, discharges, and ear mites (see p.43). Flat-faced cats are particularly prone to excess tear production, which can cause staining of the fur. Ask your vet to suggest a safe stain-removing solution.

Grooming a shorthaired cat

It takes only a few minutes of grooming to keep a short coat in perfect condition, but there is no need to rush. Be gentle and allow your cat to enjoy the attention. Follow steps 1 and 2 (see opposite), working through the coat with a wide-toothed comb and then removing debris with a slicker brush. For a salon finish, give your cat a final wipe over with a soft cloth.

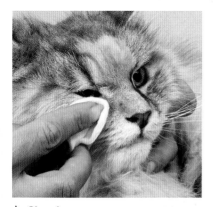

△ **Cleaning eyes**
Wipe gently around the eyes with moistened cotton wool, being careful not to touch the eyeball. Use fresh cotton wool for each eye.

△ **Cleaning ears**
Use cotton wool moistened with water or a cleaning solution formulated for cats to wipe carefully inside each ear. Never push anything into the ear canal.

Washing your cat

Cats instinctively groom themselves, keeping their fur clean, tangle-free, and conditioned. Cats may also need to be bathed occasionally to keep their coats in peak condition, especially if they are longhaired.

Outdoor cats occasionally give themselves a dust bath, rolling in dry earth to clean their coat of grease and parasites, such as fleas. You can buy dry shampoos for cats, which work in a similar way. A longhaired cat will require frequent bathing. Do not wash your cat if it is covered in oil or any other substance that is not water-soluble – instead, consult your vet. Few cats enjoy being bathed, and it's easier for both you and your cat if you accustom him to the experience from an early age. Use soothing words throughout the session. Before you begin, close all doors and windows, and make sure the room is warm.

1 △
Spraying
Brush your cat's coat before you begin. Line the bath or sink with a rubber mat so he will not slip. Slowly place your cat in, talking to him soothingly. Spray him with warm water that is as near to body temperature (38.6°C/101.5°F) as possible. Soak his fur thoroughly.

2 △
Cat shampoo
Always apply a special cat shampoo. Never use products formulated for dogs or humans, as these can contain chemicals that are an irritant or are toxic to cats. Avoid getting shampoo in your cat's eyes, ears, nose, or mouth.

3 ▷
Wash and condition
Lather in the shampoo thoroughly, then rinse it off completely. Repeat the shampoo wash or rub in a conditioner and rinse off again. Remember to keep comforting your cat throughout.

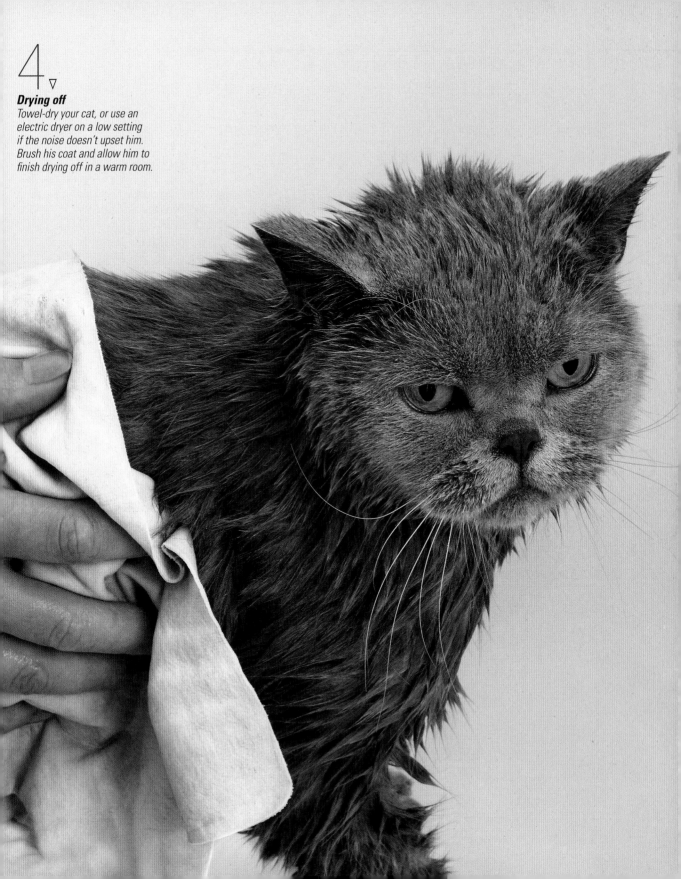

4

Drying off
Towel-dry your cat, or use an electric dryer on a low setting if the noise doesn't upset him. Brush his coat and allow him to finish drying off in a warm room.

Behavioural problems

Unacceptable behaviour – such as inappropriate scratching or soiling, or displays of aggression – needs investigating. It may be a sign that a cat has problems affecting his welfare and possibly his physical health.

Scratching

Cats scratch objects for two reasons: to maintain good claw condition and for communication. They prefer tall, sturdy objects with a vertical texture – and, unfortunately, your sofa may meet these criteria. Cats can also learn that scratching furniture attracts more attention from an owner than using a scratching post does. If your cat scratches in areas of potential conflict with other cats, such as doorways and windows, it is likely that he is leaving marks for communicative reasons, because he feels insecure there. When he is scratching furniture, you must try to identify what is worrying him and find a remedy.

To discourage a cat from scratching, cover the damaged surface with thick plastic sheeting and place a scratching post beside it. Put tasty treats on the post and make a fuss of your cat when he uses it. Once he is consistently using the post, gradually move it to a more convenient location.

Inappropriate soiling

Cats prefer to urinate and defecate in quiet, secluded locations and usually return to the same site unless it becomes unacceptable or inaccessible. For example, your cat may stop using his litter tray if it is in a noisy environment, can be disturbed by children or other pets, is too close to feeding or resting areas, is blocked by another cat, or if the type of litter has been changed. He may also be deterred by strong smells of urine if the tray has a cover or is not cleaned regularly. A change in litter tray habits can sometimes be a sign of a medical problem.

You must also determine whether your cat is relieving himself or urine-marking. Cats urine-mark in

◁ **Furniture at risk**
Scratching is a natural behaviour that gives cats exercise and helps to keep their claws in good condition. A cat may also scratch to leave his marks in certain areas where he feels insecure.

△ **Accidents happen**
Cats may soil in inappropriate places for several reasons, including a change in their environment or routine, stress caused by other cats, or because of a medical problem.

Cats are innately threatened by others that are not part of their social group. Conflicts of interest often result in fighting, especially among cats that are forced to share resources.

Aggression towards other cats is related to stress caused by a perceived, or real, threat to security. Because of their limited social communication skills, cats find it difficult to resolve conflict. Consequently, where cats cannot easily avoid other cats – for example, when they have to share a cat flap – they may fight.

Squabbles in the house can be avoided by providing each cat, or social group of cats (see p.23), with necessary resources in separate areas where they will not meet. If your cat is fighting with neighbouring cats, speak to the other owners about time-sharing, so that your cats go outside at different times and never meet. Also provide plenty of cover in your garden so that your cat can hide and feel more secure.

areas of conflict, therefore any social or environmental issues must be addressed. Ensure that there is one tray per cat, plus one extra tray. Clean soiled areas thoroughly using a safe biological agent, avoiding ammonia or other strong-smelling chemicals.

Aggression

Signals of aggression include staring, hissing, spitting, scratching, and biting. In most cases the cat has learned that aggression is necessary or effective. It is "normal" for cats to show an aggressive response, for example, if they feel threatened and are unable to escape. Aggression can also be a sign of health issues, so have your cat checked by a vet if he shows uncharacteristic behaviour.

The two main reasons for a cat's aggression towards people are fear and uninhibited play. Aggression used as a defence strategy by a frightened cat usually develops through poor socialization or a negative experience. If your cat shows signs of fear, do not try to interact with him or approach him directly. Instead, wait until he approaches you and gradually build up his confidence by using food or a toy as a reward for learning to trust you.

Aggressive play can include attacking people by grabbing them with claws and biting. High-pitched sounds or sudden movement, such as passing feet, may trigger this reaction, which generally develops through inappropriate play behaviour being permitted in kittens. Don't encourage kittens to pounce on your hands and feet. Aggressive play may also be reinforced by the "victim's" reaction – movement and noise are an invitation to further attacks and stimulate predatory instincts. Instead of responding to ambushes, ignore your cat; stay still and do not talk to or even look at him. Use your attention as a reward when he joins in a game without making you the target of his teeth and claws.

What to do if your cat has a behaviour problem

■ Have your cat's health checked by a vet to rule out underlying medical problems

■ Try to find out what first initiated the behaviour, and identify factors that trigger it now

■ If possible, protect your cat from the triggering factors

■ Never punish your cat for inappropriate behaviour or give him attention for it

■ Redirect normal cat behaviour, such as scratching, onto more appropriate targets

■ Ask your vet to refer you to a qualified and experienced feline behaviour expert

Training **and fun**

Cats are naturally active and need plenty of stimulation to ensure mental and physical well-being. Teaching good behaviour and playing games are positive ways of interacting with your cat and great fun, too.

How to train your cat

Kind, effective training involves rewarding "good" behaviour and ignoring "bad" behaviour. Never use aggressive methods as a deterrent – for example, shouting at your cat or spraying him with water. This may scare him, lead to a deterioration in his behaviour, and damage the bond between you. Build up your cat's training gradually, session by session. If you are teaching him to behave well in potentially scary situations, such as having his claws clipped or going in a cat carrier, take things very slowly and reward your cat for remaining relaxed.

Realistic expectations

Cats are motivated to perform behaviours such as hunting, climbing, jumping, and scratching – so be prepared. However, if you find any of these problematic, try to provide safe and acceptable alternatives. Never punish your cat or forceably restrain him from behaving naturally, but use physical barriers if there is a risk he might do something dangerous. You can also use indirect distraction by making an exciting noise in another room so he will stop what he is doing to investigate.

Be consistent

It is easy to be indulgent with a kitten, but bear in mind that his cute behaviour may not be acceptable in an adult cat. For example, rough and tumble or pouncing games on your hands and feet could later develop into aggressive play (see p.37). Set house rules early on – make up your mind whether you will allow your cat to sleep in your bedroom at night, sit on the tables, or climb onto shelves – and stick to your decision. If you permit the occasional lapse, your cat will never learn what is wanted of him.

◁ **Scratching post**
A post must be sturdy enough not to topple over and have a surface that will not catch claws. Some models double as activity centres.

▽ **Simple pleasures**
Cats love investigating, but also instinctively hide when they feel insecure. A simple cardboard box satisfies both of these needs.

△ **Almost the real thing**
Prevent boredom and satisfy your cat's hunting instinct by providing him with toys that mimic real prey in size, texture, and movement. Playing with you and by himself are equally important.

Keep your cat stimulated

Domestic life can frustrate a cat's natural predatory instincts, leading to a bored pet who may damage your home trying to entertain himself. Fulfil your cat's need to hunt by providing him with a satisfying substitute. Interactive toys, such as play wands with a dangling feather or a catnip mouse, give your cat something to chase and allow you to join in the fun while keeping your hands at a safe distance when he leaps on to his "prey". If he does bite during play, simply stop the game so he learns that you become boring if he bites.

Make sure you are not the sole source of fun by offering your cat toys that he can play with on his own. Toys that move or have an interesting texture are most likely to catch his attention. Rotate them regularly to prevent boredom.

Cats are also motivated to work for their food. You can buy puzzle feeders or make one yourself by cutting holes in a plastic bottle (ensuring that there are no sharp

"Make sure you are **not the sole source of fun** by offering your cat **toys** that he can **play with on his own.**"

edges) and filling it with dry food. Your cat has to paw and nose the feeder to make the food fall out. You can also scatter food around, so that he has to hunt for it instead of just eating from a bowl. Cats like to explore their environment from every angle, so provide places for your cat to investigate, perch on, or hide in: cardboard boxes and paper bags (with handles cut off) are ideal and cost nothing.

Clicker training

If you want to teach your cat behaviours – for example, going into his carrier – clicker training is very effective. A clicker is a small device with a metal tab that clicks when pressed. By clicking when your cat is doing the "right" thing, and immediately offering him a treat, you can train him to associate a click with something good and to perform the desired behaviour.

3

Your cat's
health

Signs of good health

From the very first day, get to know your cat's usual physical condition and normal behaviour so that you recognize good health and can quickly detect any signs of illness.

Healthy behaviour

- Expression bright and alert
- Runs and jumps freely
- Friendly or calm with people
- Grooms self easily
- Eats and drinks normal amounts
- Urinates and defecates normally

Appearance and behaviour

It is normal for a cat to be shy at first, but as he gets used to you his personality will emerge. In general, your cat should look alert and happy, whether he is naturally outgoing or more reserved. Note how he moves (fast or leisurely) and what sounds he makes (miaowing, chirruping). Watch how he interacts with you and your family – he should come to trust you and be happy to see you, especially once he has realized that you provide the food.

Note how your cat eats and drinks – he should have a good appetite and eat without any problem. Cats prefer to eat little and often. As they get most of their moisture from

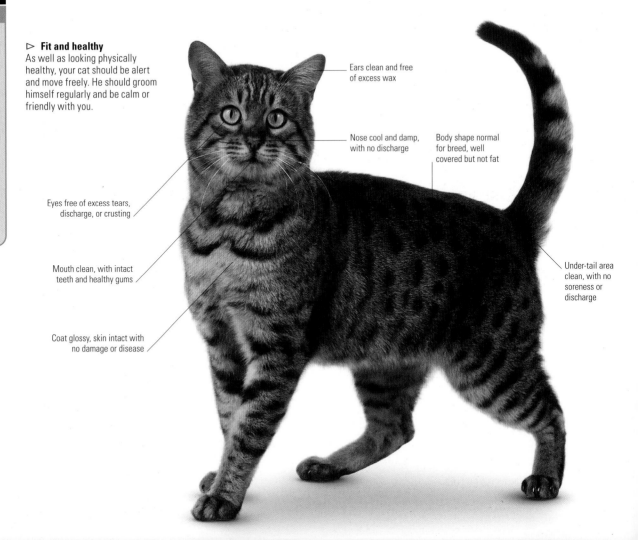

▷ **Fit and healthy**
As well as looking physically healthy, your cat should be alert and move freely. He should groom himself regularly and be calm or friendly with you.

Ears clean and free of excess wax

Nose cool and damp, with no discharge

Body shape normal for breed, well covered but not fat

Eyes free of excess tears, discharge, or crusting

Mouth clean, with intact teeth and healthy gums

Under-tail area clean, with no soreness or discharge

Coat glossy, skin intact with no damage or disease

food, cats will not drink as often as they eat, but they may drink more if fed solely on dry food.

If your cat uses a litter tray, clean it several times a day. This way you will learn how often your cat normally passes faeces and urine.

Finally, watch for unusual behaviour such as excessive licking of a body part, pawing the face, or shaking the head. These activities could suggest a wound, parasite infestation, or something stuck in the skin or coat.

Home checks

Carry out regular head-to-tail checks. With a new cat, do this every day; once you know your cat, every two or three days should be enough. If necessary, split the task into several mini-checks of a few minutes each.

> "Your cat should **look alert and happy,** whether he is **naturally outgoing or more reserved.**"

First, run your hands over your cat's head, body, and legs. Gently squeeze the abdomen to feel for lumps or sore spots. Move his legs and tail to ensure that they move freely. Feel the ribs and look at the waist to check that he is not too fat or thin.

Examine the eyes. Watch the blink rate: cats normally blink more slowly than we do. Check that the pupils respond correctly to light and dark, and that the third eyelid is barely visible. Check that the cat is not holding his ears or head at a strange angle. Look inside

Routine checks

Eyes
Check that the eyes are moist and clean. Gently pull the eyelids away from the eye; the conjunctiva (inner lining) should be pale pink.

Teeth and gums
Gently lift the lips to check the teeth and gums, and look inside the mouth. The teeth should be intact and the gums pale pink.

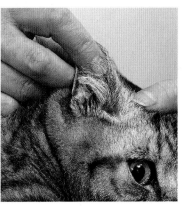

Ears
Look in the ears. The interior should be clean and pink, with no wounds, soreness, discharge, parasites, or dark wax. There should be no bad smell.

Claws
Press each paw gently to expose the claws; look for any damaged or missing claws, and then check the skin between the toes for any wounds.

the ears. Check that the nose is cool, damp, and free of excess mucus. Look inside the mouth. Check the gums for inflamed areas or bleeding. The breath should not smell bad. Press the outer gum briefly: it should go pale, but quickly turn pink when you stop.

The coat should feel smooth and not greasy. Look and feel for lumps, wounds, bald spots,

or parasites. Gently lift the scruff of the neck and then let go; the skin should quickly return to normal.

Check the claws. They should be almost totally hidden when they are retracted, and should not catch on carpets and other surfaces.

Look under the tail. The area should be clean, with no redness or swelling and no sign of worms.

Monitoring your cat's health

By monitoring your cat for changes in activity or behaviour, you can spot illness or injury at an early stage. Similarly, a vet can assess your cat's condition at regular check-ups and keep records of any problems.

◁ **Behavioural signs of illness**
If your cat seems quieter or more lethargic (weak and tired) than usual, this could signify that he is feeling ill.

hide himself away. He may be less active or may sleep more than usual. He may become abnormally timid or aggressive.

Initial visit to the vet

As soon as you have fixed the date for your cat's arrival, register with a veterinary practice, and arrange pet insurance.

If you haven't used a vet before, ask friends or neighbours for recommendations, look at local newspaper or internet advertisements, or ask an animal welfare charity or one of the cat organizations listed at the end of this book (see p.91) for suggestions on how to carry out your search.

Before making a final decision, it can help to visit local veterinary practices to find out how they are organized. Check to see if the surgery has separate access and waiting areas for cats and dogs, and

Detecting problems

Cats are notorious for hiding any signs of pain, illness, or injury. In the wild, their survival would depend on not showing weakness so that they do not attract the attention of predators. However, this ruse also means that owners might not notice problems until they have become severe.

If your cat seems more hungry or thirsty than usual, goes off his food, or loses weight, you need to consult a vet. If your cat cries or strains when passing urine or faeces, or has accidents in the home, it could signify an internal disorder.

Changes in behaviour could also indicate problems. Your cat may be reluctant to come to you or may

Signs of ill health

- Lethargy, hiding away
- Unusually fast, slow, or difficult breathing
- Sneezing or coughing
- Open wound, swelling, bleeding
- Blood in faeces, urine, or vomit
- Limping, stiffness, inability to jump onto furniture

- Unintentional weight loss
- Unexpected weight gain, especially with a bloated abdomen
- Change in appetite – eating less, walking away from food, voraciously hungry, or having difficulty eating
- Vomiting, or unexplained regurgitation of undigested food shortly after eating

- Increased thirst
- Diarrhoea, or difficulty passing a motion
- Difficulty passing urine, crying
- Itchiness
- Abnormal discharge from any orifice
- Coat changes, excessive loss of fur

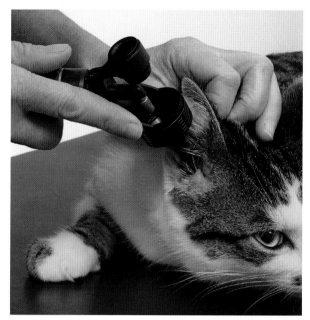

△ **Joints being checked**
A vet will feel and move your cat's limbs to detect any pain or stiffness in the joints.

◁ **Cat receiving vaccination**
Vaccination gives protection against a range of infectious diseases. Most vaccinations are given by injection.

△ **Ear check**
A vet will use an otoscope (a magnifying instrument with a light) to look inside a cat's ear canal and detect any foreign bodies, parasites, or inflammation.

allows people to put cat baskets on seats or other raised areas: arrangements that help to lessen stress for nervous pets.

A cat bought from a breeder or adopted from an animal charity

◁ **Cat being weighed**
It is important to keep accurate records of a cat's weight, especially if the cat needs to lose or gain weight.

should ideally already have had a veterinary check. Otherwise, arrange for your cat to have a full check-up as soon as you have taken ownership. The vet can check that your cat has been neutered and fitted with a microchip for identification (see Kitten health checks pp.88–9), and will carry out these procedures if needed; the vet will also assess the cat's general health, and make sure that vaccinations are up to date.

Routine vet checks
The vet will carry out basic health checks and run additional diagnostic tests if needed. You may be shown how to carry out basic checks at home (see p.43).

As well as listening to your cat's heart and counting how fast it is beating, the vet will feel for the pulse on the inside of the hind leg. He or she will watch how your cat is breathing and listen to the lungs

via a stethoscope to detect any unusual sounds such as wheezing and crackles. To measure temperature, the vet will insert a lubricated thermometer into the cat's anus.

The vet will use viewing instruments with lights to examine the interior of your cat's eyes and ears. The vet will also look inside the mouth and feel the abdomen to detect any swelling or tenderness, before moving on to examine the legs, paws, and claws.

The vet will weigh your cat. This is important as changes of even as little as 200 grams (around 7 oz) can be a symptom of ill-health in a small animal.

Additional services
Your cat should have a regular health check at least once a year. The veterinary surgery may also offer extra services such as weight control clinics, dental checks, post-neutering care, and clinics for older cats. Minor tasks such as clipping a cat's claws may be carried out by a practice nurse.

Inherited disorders

Inherited, or genetic, disorders are problems passed on from one generation to the next. There are certain disorders associated with particular breeds; a few major genetic disorders are covered here.

Why do inherited disorders occur?

Inherited disorders result from faults in genes – sections of DNA inside cells, which hold the "instructions" for the cat's development, body structures, and functions. Genetic disorders usually develop in small populations, or result from the mating of animals that are too closely related. For this reason, such disorders are more common in pedigrees. Sometimes screening tests can be used to identify cats with inherited disorders.

PKD

Polycystic kidney disease (PKD) is associated with Persian and Exotic Shorthair cats. It is an autosomal dominant disorder – that is, a cat can inherit it from just one parent. In PKD, a large number of fluid-filled cysts form in the kidneys and gradually increase in size. The disease causes increased urine production, excessive thirst, weight loss, and lethargy. Screening for PKD is possible through DNA analysis of cheek swabs.

HCM

Hypertrophic cardiomyopathy (HCM) is mainly associated with the Maine Coon and Ragdoll, and is linked to one faulty gene. The disorder causes the heart muscle to become thicker and less elastic, which reduces the space inside the heart's chambers and the volume of blood that the heart can pump. This eventually leads to heart failure. Symptoms of HCM include breathlessness, lethargy, and loss of appetite. Screening involves gene tests and ultrasound scans of the heart.

Hypokalaemic polymyopathy

This disorder is associated with Burmese, related breeds such as the Bombay and Tonkinese, and Rex cats. An autosomal recessive disorder, it is caused by faulty genes from both parents. In hypokalaemic polymyopathy, low potassium levels in the blood cause episodes of weak muscles, a stiff walk, and reduced ability to hold up the head. The cat may have difficulty breathing and standing. There is a gene test for the disorder; it can be treated with potassium supplements.

△ **Burmese cat**
Hypokalaemic polymyopathy may first appear at 2–6 months, often in Burmese or related Asian breeds. Episodes can be brought on by stress, cold weather, or exercise.

◁ **PKD and Persian cats**
Persians are one breed at risk of polycystic kidney disease. In this disorder, fluid-filled cysts develop in the kidneys, enlarging throughout the cat's life and leading to kidney failure.

Musculoskeletal disorders

The musculoskeletal system comprises bones and joints, cartilage and connective tissues, and muscles. Common musculoskeletal problems for cats are fractures and torn ligaments, but they can also develop arthritis.

Signs of a problem

- Inability to put weight on a leg
- Crying or hissing when a painful area is touched
- Swollen or misshapen body part
- Inability to jump up onto high places
- Stiffness or lameness when walking
- Reduced activity or reluctance to move
- Hiding away
- Difficulty in using a litter tray
- Reluctance to groom thoroughly

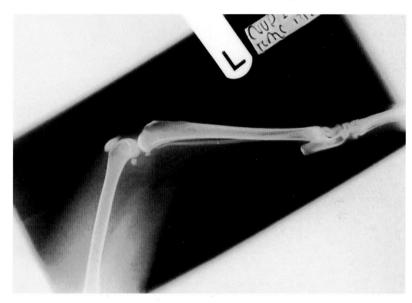

△ **Looking for injuries**
Vets commonly use radiographs to assess damage to bones and joints. The process is painless, but the cat may be sedated to keep him still.

Fractures

Broken bones in cats are most often caused by road traffic accidents (see pp.74–5); other causes include falls from high places. A break may be closed, with both bone ends inside the skin, or open (compound), with one or both broken ends protruding through the skin. The cat may be unconscious or in shock, or crying with pain. A fractured limb or tail may hang limply or at an odd angle.

Take your cat to the vet immediately. The vet will check for any internal injuries and take radiographs. The broken bone will need to be kept immobile for about 6 weeks, until it has healed. For a leg fracture, the vet may fit a cast or a splint. A serious fracture may need to be secured with implants or external fixation.

At home, you will need to keep your cat quiet and restrict his activity; you may even need to keep him in a wire crate. The vet will prescribe pain relief and he or she may fit your cat with an Elizabethan collar to stop him from licking or chewing the area.

Arthritis

The ends of bones meeting to form a joint are covered with smooth cartilage to allow ease of movement. In arthritis, the cartilage wears away and outgrowths form on the bones, leading to pain – especially during movement – and inflammation. Arthritis may be due to natural ageing, previous injury, or a developmental disorder. Obesity puts extra strain on the joints, aggravating arthritis.

Your vet will feel and move the joint and carry out radiography, and may withdraw a small sample of fluid from the joint for tests. Your cat may be referred for MRI scanning and will probably be prescribed pain relief; the vet may also advise dietary supplements for joint health and recommend a diet for weight control. At home, you will need to ensure that your cat can easily reach his food and water bowls, bed, and litter tray.

"Obesity puts extra strain on the joints, aggravating arthritis."

Eye disorders

Disorders and injuries may affect the structures of the eye or the eyelids, or both. All eye problems in a cat need prompt investigation by a vet, as even minor disorders can become sight-threatening if left untreated.

Signs of a problem

- Eyelids fully or partially closed
- Watery discharge
- Yellow/green sticky discharge
- Red inner linings of eyelids
- Cat rubbing eyes
- Increased blink rate
- Bumping into objects, misjudging heights (vision loss)
- Pupils dilated in bright light
- Swollen eyes or eyelids
- Third eyelid showing

Conjunctivitis and eye injuries

In conjunctivitis there is swelling and redness of the conjunctiva, the membrane lining the inner eyelids and covering the front of the eyes. Common causes include irritation, allergy, or infection. There may be a clear, white, or greenish discharge. The cat may blink rapidly and rub the eye. A vet may use eye drops to clear up infection and relieve inflammation, and fit an Elizabethan collar to prevent the cat from rubbing the eye.

Injury, or debris in the eye, can cause inflammation of the third eyelid and conjunctiva, or cause a bluing of the cornea at the front of the eye. A vet may use fluorescein dye to show up injury or ulceration. Treatment includes removal of debris, pain relief, and antibiotics if there is bacterial infection.

Vision loss

Loss of vision can be sudden (acute) or gradual. One cause of acute vision loss is glaucoma – a painful build-up of fluid inside the eyeball. The eyeball may look enlarged, with a widened pupil and clouded cornea. If not treated promptly, it could cause blindness. The vet will prescribe eye drops and tablets to lower the pressure.

In older cats, acute vision loss may be due to detachment of the retina. Signs include an enlarged pupil. Gradual vision loss may be due to cataracts. These can be removed surgically, and an artificial lens may be fitted.

Other eye disorders

Corneal sequestrum particularly affects Persian, Siamese, Burmese, and Himalayan cats. A dark patch of dead tissue forms on the cornea, causing pain and excess tears. The patch can be surgically removed.

Third eyelid, or haws, syndrome may result in a visible third eyelid on each eye. Possible causes include viral infection and tapeworms.

Vet checking a cat's eyes
A vet commonly uses an ophthalmoscope, an instrument with magnifying lenses and a light, to examine the interior of the eye.

△ **Cat with third eyelid syndrome**
In this condition, the third eyelid is more visible at the inner corners of both eyes. It often affects young cats.

Ear disorders

A wide range of ear problems can affect cats, from external injuries to disorders of the inner ear that can cause problems with balance. Cats can also suffer from deafness due to genetic problems.

Signs of a problem

- Shaking head
- Pawing or scratching at ear
- Smelly ear or ears
- Dirty ear or ears; dark wax or white discharge in ear
- Pain when ear is touched or when eating
- Deafness (congenital, selective)
- Swollen ear flap (haematoma)
- Head tilt, loss of balance, nausea (middle/inner ear disease)

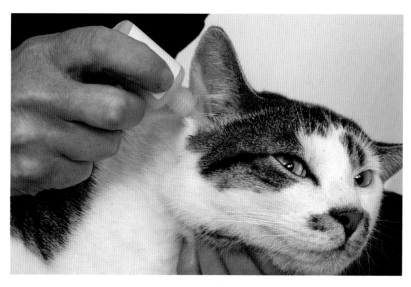

△ **Giving ear drops**
Hold the head so the ear to be treated faces upwards. Squeeze in the drops, then massage the base of the ear.

Outer ear problems

The ear flap is often injured in cat fights or by scratching. Bites or scratches may cause an abscess (an infected, pus-filled swelling) or a haematoma (a blood-filled swelling). Less commonly, skin cancer may develop, especially in cats with pale-coloured ears.

Inflammation of the ear canal (otitis externa) is commonly due to ear mites – white, dot-sized parasites (see p.52) that cause intense itching and build-up of a dark, waxy, smelly discharge. Other causes may include bacterial infections, allergies, or a tumour or a polyp (fleshy growth) in the ear canal.

Your vet may clean excess debris or discharge from the ear canal. Possible treatments include a "spot-on" treatment to eliminate ear mites, ear drops for an infection, and drainage of an abscess or a haematoma.

Middle and inner ear problems

Inflammation of the middle ear (otitis media) may result from an infection spreading down the ear canal or a foreign object piercing the eardrum. Signs include pain – causing the cat to shake its head and scratch or paw at the ear – a discharge, and lethargy. Ear infections can spread to affect nerves in the face, causing Horner's syndrome (see box, right) and pain when the cat opens its mouth.

Otitis media needs prompt attention as the infection could spread to the inner ear. This can cause hearing loss, or lead to vestibular syndrome, which interferes with balance.

Your vet may sedate or anaesthetize the cat and examine the eardrum for damage or inflammation. The vet may also arrange radiographs or an MRI scan of the inner ear.

The vet may prescribe drugs to relieve inflammation in the ear and facial nerves, antibiotics to clear up infections, or anti-nausea drugs for vestibular syndrome. A ruptured eardrum may heal by itself, but for persistent otitis media, surgery may be needed to drain pus.

Horner's syndrome

Ear infection may spread to the facial nerves, leading to Horner's syndrome in the eye on that side. Symptoms include:

- Sunken eyeball
- Constricted pupil
- Drooping lower eyelid
- Visible third eyelid

Coat and skin disorders

Cats by nature keep their coat and skin healthy by grooming themselves. However, skin disorders can still affect them. Such problems are usually easy to spot, and will need prompt attention from a vet.

Signs of a problem

- Dull, greasy coat
- Scaly, scabby, or crusty bits on skin and in coat
- Skin rash or spots
- Hair loss
- Colour change
- Itchiness with excessive licking or scratching
- Unpleasant smell from coat
- "Hot cat" (cat whose skin feels burning hot)
- Bumps or lumps

Allergy

Allergic skin conditions can occur when your cat's immune system, which protects the body from infection, overreacts to a certain substance, such as a type of food, pollen, or parasite (see pp.52–3). Signs could include many of those listed in the box (left). In a reaction known as miliary dermatitis, the skin breaks out in little bumps, scabs, and crusts, usually along the back and at the base of the tail. This condition often progresses to weeping areas of infected skin that need to be treated with an extended course of antibiotics.

The commonest cause of allergic skin disease and miliary dermatitis is a hypersensitivity to fleas. Your vet will check for infestation by running a fine-toothed comb through your cat's coat and may take skin scrapings for microscopic examination. If your vet suspects that your cat's allergy is caused by certain foods, he or she may advise a hypoallergenic diet for a few weeks, and then gradually reintroduce the original diet to try to identify triggers. Treatment of allergies may include drugs such as corticosteroid or cyclosporine, or a course of desensitizing vaccine. Antihistamines or omega-3 fatty acids may also be helpful.

Ringworm

This fungal infection is highly contagious and can be transmitted to or from humans as well as between animals. In cats it may cause grey, scaly, crusty areas on the skin and patches of fur loss, commonly on the head, ears, back, or paws. However, there may be no signs at all, and ringworm may not be diagnosed until a person in contact with the cat develops an itchy skin lesion (the infection rarely causes itching in cats).

To make a diagnosis, the vet will examine the cat's hair using an ultraviolet lamp (Wood's lamp). Areas of hair infected by ringworm sometimes, but not always, glow

◁ **Excessive scratching**
Scratching may further aggravate itchy skin, and the cat's claws can infect the area with bacteria.

△ **Severe fur loss**
Cats naturally have areas of thin fur just in front of the ears, but thin or bald patches anywhere else are a cause for concern.

▷ **Incessant licking**
Cats may lick themselves excessively if they have itchy or sore skin. Over-grooming may also be a sign of anxiety or stress.

green. Your vet will also collect a sample of hairs for fungal culture. All other pets in your home should be tested as well.

Ringworm is usually treated with an oral antifungal drug, coupled with an antifungal shampoo. The fungal spores can stay in your home for months, so you will need to disinfect or replace items such as grooming equipment and bedding, and thoroughly vacuum floors and furniture, carefully disposing of the vacuum's contents. Long-haired cats may need to be clipped to reduce the risk of further contamination.

Cat bite abscess

An abscess is a swelling filled with pus. Abscesses often result from fights with other cats, as teeth may transmit infection into the wound. Your cat may become feverish, lose his appetite, and hide away.

If the swelling bursts, your cat will feel better. You will need to bathe the area with a teaspoonful of salt in half a litre of water, and take the cat to the vet. If the abscess has not yet burst, the vet

may lance it to release the pus. The vet will prescribe antibiotics for the infection, and advise you to keep cleaning the area until the abscess has healed.

Acne and stud tail

Both of these conditions arise from over-production of oily sebum from glands in the skin. Acne most often occurs on the chin; stud tail affects the base of the tail, resulting in a greasy, often matted, patch of fur. Stud tail mostly, but not exclusively, occurs in unneutered males.

Generally, these are cosmetic conditions but sometimes an area becomes infected and needs treating with antibiotics. To improve stud tail, your vet may clip away the fur and prescribe a wash to reduce greasiness. If your cat is an unneutered male, the vet will recommend castration.

Skin growths

If you find a lump on your cat, always have it investigated promptly. Your vet may take a sample of cells for analysis, either with a needle while your cat is conscious, or as a biopsy under a general anaesthetic. If a serious problem – for example, a cancerous growth – is diagnosed, your vet will discuss the options with you.

Unpigmented or light skin on areas such as ears, eyelids, lips, and nose is prone to skin cancer. If your cat develops ulcerated, crusty, or sore patches in these areas, have him examined by a vet as soon as possible. Treatment of skin cancer has the best chance of success when carried out at an early stage. As a preventive measure, you can use high-factor sunscreens that are specifically formulated for cats and resistant to washing and grooming.

"If you find a **lump** on your cat, always have it **investigated promptly.**"

External parasites

External parasites, or ectoparasites, are tiny creatures that infest a cat's skin, such as fleas, ticks, and mites. Saliva from their bites can irritate the skin, and the parasites can also transmit disease.

Signs of a problem

- Thinning of the fur, patches of bare skin
- Scabs and crusting
- Itching, discomfort
- Over-grooming
- Shaking head
- Itchy skin lesions on owners or other pets
- May see actual parasite

Fleas

The most common external parasite is the flea, which feeds on blood. Heavy infestation in kittens can cause anaemia due to blood loss. In some cats, flea saliva may trigger dermatitis (see p.51) or a severe allergic reaction. Fleas may also pass on tapeworms (see opposite) and transmit diseases such as bartonellosis (cat scratch disease) between cats.

A cat with fleas may scratch and groom himself excessively, causing hair loss and inflamed or broken skin. You may see fleas or black specks (flea faeces) in the fur. Other pets or humans may be bitten.

Your vet can recommend a treatment for effective flea control. You will need to treat any other pets that you have, and you may have to spray your carpets, furniture, and car. Never treat your cat with products designed for dogs; these can be toxic to cats.

Ticks

Like fleas, ticks feed on blood – but they are much larger. These eight-legged creatures are most commonly found in moorland, long grass, or woodland, mainly in spring or autumn. They hold on to the skin and feed with their mouthparts. They look like grey pimples that grow larger as the ticks feed. Ticks can cause anaemia due to blood loss, and the mouthparts can irritate the skin. Ticks can also pass on bacterial and other infections, some of which can be serious – such as Lyme disease and tularaemia (rabbit fever).

Your vet can show you how to remove a tick using a tick hook, twisting gently to persuade the tick to let go to ensure that the mouthparts are not left behind. To prevent infestation, ask your vet for advice on tick-repellent products.

Mites

Several species of these tiny creatures may infest cats. Ear mites (see p.49) are one common

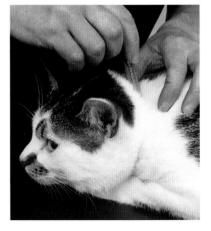

△ **Checking a cat for fleas**
Using a fine-toothed flea comb, especially on the neck and the base of the tail, may help you find fleas or flea faeces.

form. Bright orange harvest mites, which feed on tissue fluid, are another. These can cause intense itching, and pimples or crusting, on thinly furred areas such as the head in front of the ears and between the toes. Other species include *Cheyletiella* mites, or "walking dandruff", and the head mite *Notoedres cati*. The latter causes feline scabies, an uncommon but serious condition that results in itching and raw, crusted, thickened skin. A vet may take skin scrapings to identify the mites and recommend species-specific treatment.

▷ **Parasites**
Four common external parasites are shown here. Cats may easily pick up these parasites from their outdoor environment or from other cats.

Flea

Tick

Ear mite

Harvest mite

Internal parasites

Some parasites live in a cat's internal body tissues, usually in the intestines but sometimes in other areas such as the lungs. The three most common types are roundworms, tapeworms, and *Toxoplasma*.

Signs of a problem

- ■ Constant hunger but loss of weight
- ■ Bloated belly
- ■ Diarrhoea
- ■ Coughing
- ■ General ill-health
- ■ Rough or dull coat
- ■ Adult worms seen in vomit or faeces
- ■ Tapeworm segments seen on or under the tail, or in faeces

Roundworm

The most common internal parasites are roundworms, which look like strands of spaghetti. They live in the gut, and their eggs are passed in faeces. Cats may swallow eggs from infested prey or after contact with faeces. Nursing mothers may pass larvae to their kittens through their milk. There is also a risk of *Toxocara* roundworms being passed to humans.

Roundworms absorb nutrients from the cat's food and can damage the gut lining. Signs include loss of condition, vomiting, diarrhoea, and a pot belly. Kittens may be more severely affected than adults. Heavy worm infestations may block the intestines. Larvae can cause coughing when they migrate through the lung.

If your cat has roundworms, your vet may examine the cat's faecal sample. Your pet will be prescribed a deworming drug. You will also be advised on preventative medication.

Tapeworm

Cats usually pick up tapeworms by swallowing fleas (which can carry tapeworm eggs) while grooming themselves, or by eating worm-infested prey. The worms grow in the cat's gut, absorbing nutrients from food. Tapeworm infestation can be a cause of vomiting and weight loss.

Adult worms shed flat body segments containing eggs, which the cat passes in its faeces. These look like wriggly rice grains around the anus, on the tail, or in faeces. Your vet will prescribe an anti-tapeworm drug. Strict flea control can help to prevent reinfestation.

Toxoplasmosis

Infection with the single-celled organism *Toxoplasma gondii* is called toxoplasmosis. Cats may pick up the organism from infected prey; they also pass oocysts (immature

△ **Worms and weight loss**
Worm infestation can cause a cat to lose weight because the worms take nutrients from the cat's food as it passes through the intestine.

organisms) in their faeces. It is sensible for a pregnant woman to wear gloves when handling cat litter to prevent the risk of passing toxoplasmosis to her unborn baby.

Few cats show signs of toxoplasmosis, but some develop fever, inflammation in the eye, nervous system problems, vomiting, and diarrhoea. Toxoplasmosis is usually treated with an antibiotic called clindamycin.

▷ **Roundworm**
Roundworms can grow up to 10 cm (4 inches) long, and range in colour from white to pale brown. Roundworm eggs can remain infective for months or even years.

Mouth and tooth disorders

Cats use their mouths for eating and for grooming themselves. The mouth usually keeps itself healthy by producing saliva, but regular checks and even brushing the teeth will help prevent problems.

Signs of a problem

- Bad breath (halitosis)
- Yellow or brown discoloration of teeth
- White or yellow deposit (plaque) at base of teeth
- Red gumline at base of teeth
- Difficulty eating; possible avoidance of some foods
- Loss of appetite
- Crying in pain when trying to eat, or pawing at mouth
- Drooling saliva, pus, or blood
- Swelling on side of face
- Grey discharge at gumline (pus)
- Growth inside mouth or on jaws

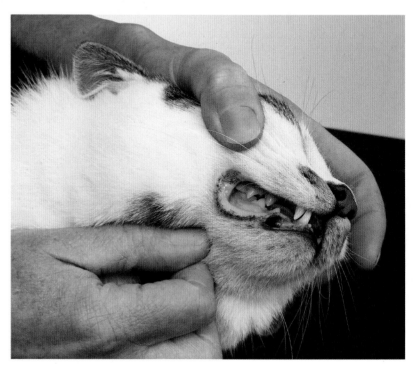

△ **Vet checking teeth**
Your vet will examine the cat's teeth, gums, and lining of the mouth for problems such as tartar, gingivitis, bleeding, or injuries.

Keeping teeth healthy

It is important to check your cat's mouth regularly (see p.43) and keep the teeth clean to prevent the build-up of plaque. This is a sticky film consisting of bacteria and food debris, which builds up after eating. Over time it can mix with minerals in the saliva, forming a hard, yellowish brown deposit called tartar (calculus).

Your vet may be able to suggest anti-plaque foods or additives. Brushing your cat's teeth at least once a week can also help. You need to use special cat toothpaste – never human toothpaste – and a cat toothbrush (or wrap your fingertip in gauze). Lift the lips gently, then brush or massage along the teeth and gumline.

Gingivitis and stomatitis

Disorders such as gingivitis (inflamed gums) and stomatitis (inflammation inside the mouth) are most often caused by the cat's immune system reacting against bacteria in plaque. Other causes include infectious diseases such as feline calicivirus (FCV). Stomatitis can also be due to a foreign body lodged in the mouth or a reaction to a household chemical.

In gingivitis the gumline is dark red. If left untreated, the gums may recede or separate from the teeth, leaving inflamed pockets where infection can take hold (periodontitis). In stomatitis the inside of the mouth is red and sore. In both cases the cat may be in obvious pain (see box, above),

drool, and have difficulty eating or avoid certain foods. In severe cases, teeth may become loose or fall out altogether.

Your vet may anaesthetise your cat to remove tartar with an ultrasonic descaler and to polish the teeth. Loose and diseased teeth are likely to be removed. Antibiotics are usually prescribed to clear up infection, along with a pain-killing drug.

Dental abscess

This is a pus-filled swelling that develops at the root of a tooth, due to infection entering the tissues. It

may be very painful, causing the cat to paw at his face. Your cat may struggle to eat or may try to eat with just one side of his mouth. He may avoid hard foods or lose his appetite, drool, and have bad breath. You may see grey pus at the gumline, or a lump under the skin on the cheek.

The vet may anaesthetize your cat before looking in the mouth and taking radiographs. Your cat may be prescribed antibiotics and pain relief, but if the abscess is severe the tooth may be extracted.

> "Use a **special cat toothpaste** and a cat toothbrush to **clean your cat's teeth.**"

Malocclusion
In malocclusion the teeth are misaligned and do not fit together properly when the cat closes its mouth. It can result from injury to the jaw or from overcrowded teeth. Malocclusion can interfere with eating and can also trap food and plaque, increasing the risk of infections. Certain short-nosed breeds, such as Persians, may have jaws too short to fit all the teeth. In some cats, when adult teeth come through baby teeth do not fall out, so the adult teeth grow crooked. Your vet may extract the misaligned teeth.

Growths
The most common type of tumour (growth) in the mouth is squamous cell carcinoma, a form of cancer. It grows from the cells lining the mouth and throat and most often arises under the tongue or in the gums. Older cats are most at risk. A tumour may be seen as a nodule or a lumpy mass. Your cat may have bad breath, drooling, and bleeding or ulcers in the mouth, and may find it hard to swallow or close the mouth. The cat may develop loose teeth or a distorted face.

Tumours grow fast and need prompt attention. Your vet may radiograph the cat's head and take a tissue sample from the growth to identify the tumour. Treatment may involve surgery to remove the tumour and radiotherapy to kill remaining cancer cells. The tumours often recur, so your cat will need regular monitoring.

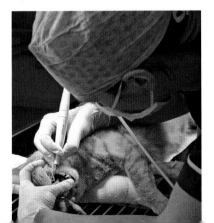

◁ **Vet performing dental work**
The canines are the baby teeth most commonly retained as the adult teeth grow. A vet may need to extract the baby teeth so the adult teeth will grow straight.

Home care after dental treatment
After a dental procedure, your cat may have a sore mouth, and as he will have had a general anaesthetic he will be groggy for a while. Your vet will prescribe pain relief and may provide a diet plan consisting of foods that are easy to eat. Put your cat's bed in a quiet place, with food, water, and a litter tray within easy reach. You may need to hand-feed him until he can eat by himself.

Digestive disorders

The digestive system breaks down food, releasing nutrients to be converted into energy by the body's cells. Any problem with your cat's eating or digestion can have an overall impact on health.

Signs of a problem

- Vomiting or regurgitation
- Increase or decrease in appetite
- Constipation – inability to defecate, lasting more than a day
- Diarrhoea – frequently passing large volumes of loose faeces
- Blood in faeces
- Stools (faeces) of altered colour, frequency, or consistency
- Weight loss

▽ **General illness**
A cat with vomiting or diarrhoea may seem abnormally quiet and lethargic. He may be lacking energy due to dehydration and a lack of nutrients.

Changes in appetite

Loss of appetite may indicate a sore mouth (see pp.54-5), cat flu (see p.58), a gastrointestinal disorder, or an illness such as kidney disease (see p.67). Stress may also make a cat reluctant to eat. Try tempting your cat with tasty foods, and call the vet. Do not let your cat go for more than a day without eating, as this can endanger his health.

A significant increase in appetite can also be a sign of illness, such as hyperthyroidism (see p.61), or a side effect of certain drugs, such as corticosteroids. Even if there is no obvious cause, you need to monitor your cat's weight, as obesity can produce or worsen health problems.

Vomiting and regurgitation

Vomiting is a cat's way of protecting himself against bad food or poisons (see pp.78-9). It is normal for a healthy cat to vomit occasionally, such as after consuming grass or to eliminate hairballs. A single episode of vomiting is no cause for alarm. However, repeated vomiting can be a sign of illness, or of a hairball or other object blocking the stomach or intestine, and you should contact your vet.

Repeated vomiting and abdominal pain indicate a serious digestive disorder that may have been caused by eating an irritant or contaminated food. Persistent

△ **Tempting the appetite**
If your cat has gone off his food, try offering a few tasty treats such as prawns. Serve food at room temperature or warm it up a little to make it smell more appetizing.

vomiting can result in dehydration. Offer a tiny amount of bland food and a little water every hour but seek urgent veterinary attention if your kitten or cat continues to vomit.

Regurgitation is "sicking up" of food shortly after eating. The food will be slimy but relatively unaltered in appearance. (By contrast, vomiting is the expulsion of partially digested food.) Occasional regurgitation is not a problem but, if it happens repeatedly, it could indicate a blockage in the throat or the oesophagus (gullet), which will need veterinary attention.

Diarrhoea

Like vomiting, diarrhoea is a natural way for a cat's body to expel harmful substances. After a single bout, offer tiny amounts of bland food every hour but give plenty of water.

> "Severe or persistent diarrhoea **can be dangerous**, leaving your cat **weak and dehydrated.**"

Repeated episodes of diarrhoea may indicate parasite infestation (see p.53), a digestive problem, or an underlying disorder such as kidney or liver disease. Drugs, such as some antibiotics, can also cause diarrhoea as a side effect. Get in touch with your vet if your cat suffers from severe or persistent diarrhoea as it can be dangerous, leaving your cat weak and dehydrated. One common cause of diarrhoea is a rapid change in diet. Introduce any new food

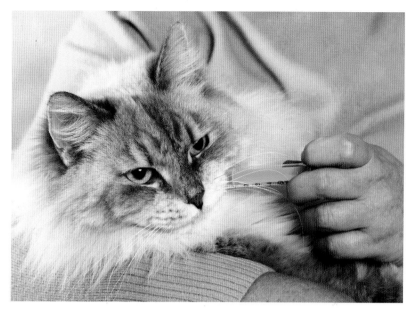

△ **Medicine for constipation**
Laxatives, which relieve constipation, may be supplied as a paste, gel, or liquid, which you feed to the cat on your finger or by syringe. Only give medicines prescribed by a vet.

gradually, by mixing it with the original food in increasing proportions, so that the gut can adjust to it. Another common problem is intolerance to lactose, a sugar in cows' milk. Avoid giving milk – adult cats do not need it, and young kittens should have only their mother's milk.

Constipation

A healthy cat should defecate about once a day. Constipation is the infrequent passing of faeces, or passing of hard, dry stools. It is common in older cats, especially those that swallow a lot of hair when grooming. Other causes include dehydration, a spine or pelvic injury, or a nerve disorder.

A constipated cat may crouch repeatedly but fail to pass faeces. If the problem persists for more than a day, the cat may lose his appetite, look weak and uncomfortable, and vomit. You will need to take your

cat to the vet, who may detect a constipated bowel when examining his abdomen. The vet may also radiograph the intestines and carry out blood and urine tests to determine the cause of the constipation. Treatment depends on the cause. Often, the vet will prescribe a laxative. Severe cases may need surgery or an enema.

Dangers of gastroenteritis

Gastroenteritis is inflammation of the stomach and intestinal lining. It may be caused by parasite infestation (see p.53), infection, such as feline panleukopenia (see p.64), or an immune system reaction. Some cases are mild, but severe cases may result in profuse vomiting, "dry heaving" (where the cat tries to vomit but nothing comes up), and diarrhoea. The cat may become dangerously dehydrated, and there may be blood in the vomit or diarrhoea. If your cat develops gastroenteritis, contact your vet. In the event of a severe case, call the vet urgently.

Respiratory disorders

The respiratory system extends from the nose and mouth to the lungs. Disorders can vary from common ailments such as sneezing and a runny nose to serious conditions that can interfere with your cat's breathing.

Signs of a problem

- Nasal discharge from one or both nostrils: watery, white or green, or blood
- Sneezing
- Cough (fluid and "chesty" or dry and harsh)
- Increased rate of breathing
- Breathing with mouth open, panting
- Noisy breathing or wheezing
- Difficulty in breathing – sitting hunched with neck stretched out
- Anorexia, weight loss, dehydration
- Lethargy

Cat flu

Most cases of cat flu are due to feline calicivirus (FCV) or feline herpesvirus (FHV). Highly contagious, cat flu may be transmitted both by sick animals and by seemingly unaffected carriers.

Signs include fever, sneezing, runny eyes and nose, open-mouthed breathing, or a very sore throat causing loss of appetite, dehydration, and lethargy. FCV can cause mouth ulcers and gingivitis (see p.54), resulting in drooling. FHV can cause conjunctivitis and ulcers on the cornea.

Cats should be vaccinated against FCV and FHV. If your cat does develop signs of cat flu, call your vet. For viral infections, the only treatment is to provide relief by keeping the nose and eyes clean and perhaps placing the cat in a steamy bathroom to ease breathing. Keep your cat isolated and wash your hands after handling him, to avoid spreading the infection.

Feline asthma

In asthma, inhaled allergens such as pollen, dust, or cigarette smoke can irritate the tiny airways in the lungs, inflaming them so they produce more mucus. The cat may have persistent dry coughing, wheezing, and lethargy. A cat can also suffer asthma attacks, in which the airways suddenly contract. He will sit hunched up, panting or gasping for breath. Gums and lips may turn blue. This needs immediate veterinary attention.

The vet may give oxygen to relieve an attack. Your cat may be prescribed corticosteroids to reduce inflammation and bronchodilator drugs to relax the airways.

△ **Flu spreading between cats**
Cat flu can be spread easily by direct contact between cats, or transmitted on hands, clothing, or objects such as feeding bowls.

Reducing exposure to allergens can help prevent attacks, and shedding excess weight can ease breathing.

Pyothorax

This rare but life-threatening condition is caused by a bacterial (or occasionally fungal) infection in the chest cavity, which leads to a build-up of pus and fluid around the lungs. The fluid compresses the lungs, causing the cat to breathe shallowly or struggle for breath. The cat may have a fever, and the gums and lips may turn blue. This needs urgent veterinary attention.

The vet will drain the fluid; this may take several days. Your cat will also be prescribed a course of antibiotics to clear the infection.

Heart and blood disorders

The heart pumps blood around the body, and this blood carries oxygen to all body tissues. Problems with a cat's heart, blood vessels, or red blood cells can cause weakness or even make the cat collapse.

Signs of a problem

- Difficulty in breathing
- Blue lips, gums, and tongue
- Fatigue, lethargy
- Anorexia, weight loss
- Increased thirst
- Fainting
- Hindlimb pain and loss of use
- Cough (rare)

Cardiomyopathy

This disease weakens the heart muscle. The most common form is hypertrophic cardiomyopathy (HCM), which causes the heart's left ventricle (lower chamber) to enlarge and stiffen. Blood may clot in the heart, and bits of clot may lodge in an artery. This can be life-threatening. Causes of HCM include a genetic defect (see p.46), hypertension (see below), or hyperthyroidism (see p.61).

The cat may tire easily, breathe heavily, and lose his appetite. The vet will use a stethoscope to listen to the heart sounds, and carry out radiographs, ultrasound scans, and ECG. The vet may give drugs to regulate the heartbeat, relax the blood vessels, and eliminate excess fluid from the body.

Hypertension

Raised blood pressure, or hypertension, usually results from other disorders such as hyperthyroidism or kidney disease (see p.67) and most often affects older cats. The pressure can damage the smallest blood vessels, making them bleed. This can cause serious problems such as vision loss, kidney damage, and seizures. The heart also has to work harder, so the cat becomes easily tired and breathless. The cat will need to see a vet, who will measure the blood pressure, give anti-hypertensive drugs, and treat any underlying cause.

Anaemia

In anaemia, the blood has too few red blood cells, which carry oxygen to the body tissues. Causes include injuries, parasite infestations (see pp.52–3), immune system disorders (see pp.62–3), feline infectious anaemia, or kidney disease. The lack of oxygen causes pale gums, tiring easily, and laboured breathing. Blood tests may be performed to diagnose the underlying cause, which will determine the treatment.

△ **Vet listening to a cat's heartbeat**
Vets use a stethoscope to listen to a cat's heartbeat and breathing rate, and to detect any unusual noises in the chest.

▷ **Vet taking a cat's blood pressure**
Usually only the systolic phase of the blood pressure (as the heart muscle contracts) is measured. Any reading over 160mmHg shows hypertension.

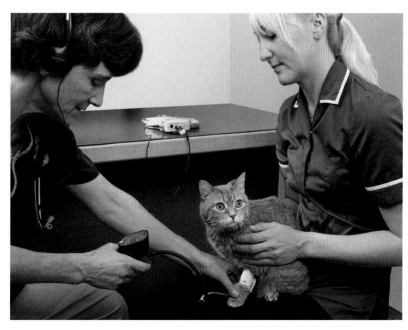

Nervous system disorders

The nervous system, comprising the brain, spinal cord, and nerves, carries electrical signals that control body functions and conscious activities. Injuries, genetic disorders, and infections are some of the main causes of problems.

Signs of a problem

- Fits
- Disorientation
- Behavioural changes
- Head tilt
- Poor balance

Seizures and epilepsy

In a seizure, abnormal electrical activity in the cat's brain may cause collapse, foaming at the mouth, and jerking body and legs. A cat may also show a violent, unprovoked behaviour change such as lashing out in rage. The most common cause is poisoning (see pp.78–9). Other causes include head injury, stroke, tumour, or infection.

Recurrent seizures with no obvious cause are known as epilepsy. Seizures need prompt veterinary attention. A vet will carry out blood tests and may advise radiography, CT scans, or MRI scans of the brain. Your cat will be treated for any underlying problem. If the cat has epilepsy, he may need anti-epileptic drugs for life.

Inherited and congenital disorders

Certain nervous system problems are genetic (see p.46). For example, the gene that produces white fur and blue eyes may also cause deafness. In Manx cats, the gene that causes them to be born tailless may also produce defects in the spinal cord. Some other disorders are congenital (present from birth).

△ **Movement problems in kittens**
Young kittens can be wobbly on their feet at first, but a kitten exposed to panleukopenia virus while in the womb may move in a jerky, clumsy way.

For example, if a pregnant cat catches panleukopenia (feline infectious enteritis), her kittens may be born with brain damage that causes trembling and a jerky, wide-legged walking gait. Cats are usually vaccinated against panleukopenia.

Vestibular syndrome

The vestibular apparatus in the inner ear controls balance. Problems with this area, or the nerve connecting it to the brain, may cause a cat to fall over, totter in circles, or crouch when he walks. Other signs may include a head tilt, eyes flicking from side to side, nausea, and vomiting. In most cases no cause can be found, but sometimes the disorder results from an ear infection (see p.49) or, more rarely, a brain tumour or stroke. A vet may treat underlying problems and symptoms such as nausea, but usually the condition clears up by itself in a few days.

◁ **Blood tests**
The vet may take blood samples to detect any underlying illness that could be causing seizures.

Hormonal disorders

Hormones are body chemicals that control particular functions. They are produced by glands and carried in the bloodstream to the places where they are needed. Any over- or underproduction of hormones may cause disorders.

Hyperthyroidism

The thyroid gland produces the hormones that control metabolism – the speed at which the body's functions occur. Hyperthyroidism, or overproduction of thyroid hormones, causes the metabolism to speed up. This condition is very common and most often affects older cats.

The cat may be ravenously hungry but still lose weight, and drink and urinate more than normal. Other signs include vomiting and diarrhoea. You may be able to feel a rapid, thumping heartbeat. The fur may become dull and untidy. The cat may be restless and excitable, or in some cases lethargic. If untreated, hyperthyroidism may lead to hypertension and heart failure (see p.59).

A vet may feel for an enlarged thyroid in the neck, listen for a heart murmur (abnormal heart sound), measure the blood pressure, and take blood and urine samples. The vet may prescribe drugs or a low-iodine diet to reduce the production of thyroid hormones. The cat will need to follow these for life. Other possible treatments are surgery to remove the thyroid tissue or radiotherapy to destroy abnormal thyroid cells.

Diabetes mellitus

The pancreas secretes insulin to control how the body's cells take in glucose – the main form of energy from food. In diabetes mellitus the pancreas produces too little insulin, or the cells do not respond to it. As a result, blood glucose levels become too high, while the cells cannot obtain enough energy. Diabetes mellitus is most common in middle-aged or older cats, especially if overweight.

◁ **Signs of a thyroid problem**
Most cats with hyperthyroidism become restless and excitable, but some may become weak and lethargic and lose their appetite.

△ **Overweight cat**
Being overweight and having an inactive lifestyle are two of the main factors that increase the risk of a cat developing diabetes.

An affected cat may be ravenously hungry but still lose weight. Excess glucose in the urine may cause the cat to urinate more than usual and become very thirsty to compensate for the fluid loss. It may also predispose to bladder infections. Over time, excess blood glucose can irritate nerves and blood vessels, damaging the brain, nerves, eyes, and kidneys.

A vet will collect blood and urine samples to detect excess glucose. Diabetes can usually be controlled with insulin injections once or twice a day. Your vet will show you how to give these. The vet may also prescribe a low carbohydrate/high protein diet, and advise on weight control if the cat is overweight.

Immune system disorders

The immune system fights infections and diseases. Disorders arise if the system is weakened, or conversely if it is overstimulated by normally harmless substances, or overreacts and attacks the body's own tissues.

Allergies

These arise when the immune system overreacts to substances in the environment that are usually harmless, such as dust, pollen, chemicals, and some foods. Flea bites are one of the most common causes of allergies. All of these substances contain molecules known as allergens. Cats often develop allergies when young and may have them for life.

Allergies most often affect the skin, making it itchy and inflamed. Cats may scratch or groom themselves excessively, causing hair loss and sore or broken skin (see p.51). Direct contact with allergens can cause conjunctivitis (see p.48). Food allergies can cause vomiting as well as itching. Inhaled allergens can cause asthma (see p.58). Insect bites or stings (see p.77) can cause severe skin irritation or even a dangerous reaction called anaphylaxis.

A vet may carry out skin or blood tests to identify substances that trigger allergies. The main treatment is to remove or minimize allergens in the environment – for example, eliminating fleas, or changing the diet to avoid foods that trigger reactions. The vet may also prescribe medications such as low-dose corticosteroids or cyclosporine, to control allergic reactions. In some cases, a course of injections may be given to desensitize your cat to one or more allergens identified, but this treatment may need to be continued for some time.

Eosinophilic granuloma complex

This term refers to a group of severe allergic skin reactions caused by overactivity of eosinophils – white blood cells that normally respond to allergens or fight off parasites. The saliva from flea, mosquito, or mite bites (see p.52) is a common cause of these reactions. Other causes include food or inhaled allergens.

The reactions cause three main types of sore. Granulomas are lumpy or ridge-like sores that most

◁ **Scratching and over-grooming**
Allergens most often produce skin irritation or inflammation in cats, leading to repeated scratching, rubbing of the eyes, or excessive licking and chewing of the skin.

▽ **Microscopic examination**
To help identify skin disorders, a vet may scrape a sample of cells from an affected area of the skin and examine them under a microscope to detect abnormalities.

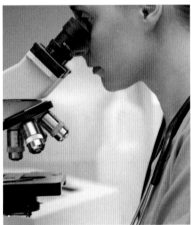

often occur on the hind legs or paws, or inside the mouth. Plaques are flat, red, thickened areas of bare skin, often on the abdomen or inner thighs. Ulcers (or rodent ulcers) are raw areas, often with a raised border, that usually develop on the upper lip. Mosquito bite hypersensitivity may lead to sores on the nose, ears, and pads of the paws. The cat may scratch or lick sores, possibly breaking the skin and causing infection.

A vet may take samples from the sores to confirm the diagnosis, and may prescribe corticosteroids to reduce inflammation and antibiotics to clear up any secondary bacterial infection. You will need to prevent exposure to allergens – for example, keeping your cat indoors to avoid mosquitoes, or eliminating fleas.

Lymphoma

One of the most common forms of cancer in cats, lymphoma arises in the lymphatic system. This system carries lymphocytes – white blood cells that fight infectious organisms. These cells collect in tiny, bean-shaped lymph nodes (which also trap disease organisms and cancerous cells).

Lymphoma has three main forms. Alimentary (intestinal) lymphoma, the most common, causes weight loss, vomiting, diarrhoea, and enlarged lymph nodes in the abdomen. Mediastinal lymphoma develops in the chest. Signs include difficulty in breathing and regurgitation of food. Multicentric lymphoma involves lymph nodes throughout the body. Swollen nodes may be felt under the jaw and in the armpits and groin. Cats carrying feline leukaemia virus (FeLV) or feline immunodeficiency virus (FIV) are at a greater risk of lymphoma as their immune system is already weakened. Immunization against FeLV can reduce the risk of lymphoma in cats.

A vet will test the cat for FeLV and FIV, carry out blood tests, and take biopsies of enlarged lymph nodes. Treatment may involve surgery, radiotherapy, or chemotherapy, depending on the location and size of tumours. There is no cure, but treatment may prolong life.

Pemphigus

This refers to a group of skin disorders in which the cat's immune system attacks the skin tissues. This causes scaly or crusty areas, fluid-filled blisters, and ulcers. These usually develop on the head, ears, and pads of the paws, and in some cases on the gums and lips. The sores are itchy and painful. A vet may take skin samples from the sores to identify the disease, and prescribe corticosteroids and immunosuppressant drugs to reduce the disease activity.

Infectious diseases

Your cat may catch infectious diseases from the environment or from other cats. These diseases can be serious, especially in old cats or kittens, but vaccination can help to protect your pet.

Feline panleukopenia

This disease, caused by feline parvovirus, is also called feline infectious enteritis or feline distemper. It easily spreads between cats or is picked up from the environment. The virus attacks the white blood cells, weakening the immune system. It causes gastroenteritis, resulting in fever, pain when drinking, vomiting or diarrhoea, dehydration, and possibly death. If kittens are infected just before or after birth they may die or suffer cerebellar hypoplasia, a form of brain damage. Vets routinely vaccinate cats against this disease.

FHV and FCV

Feline herpes virus (FHV) and feline calicivirus (FCV) cause up to 90 per cent of upper respiratory infections, or "cat flu" (see p.58). Infected cats may spread the virus by sneezing, coughing, or licking objects or other cats. Even when they have recovered from the flu, cats may still carry the virus and pass it to others. They are especially likely to share the herpes virus when ill or stressed. Vets routinely vaccinate cats against FHV and FCV. Vaccination will not prevent the diseases, but it can make the signs less severe.

Chlamydophila felis

The bacterium *Chlamydophila felis* mainly causes conjunctivitis (see p.48), with sore, inflamed inner eyelids, and excess tears. It can also cause mild cat flu. It is passed on by direct contact and most often affects kittens or unvaccinated adults living in groups. Vets treat the infection with antibiotics. They may advise vaccination for cats living in groups.

▽ **Passing on infection**
Cats kept in large groups or close contact can pick up infections from mutual grooming, fighting, or sharing objects such as feeding bowls.

FeLV

A potentially deadly virus, feline leukaemia virus (FeLV) is shed in saliva, other body fluids, and faeces. Pregnant or nursing cats can pass it to their kittens. Some cats may overcome the virus, but it may take hold in kittens or in cats that are already sick. The virus attacks the immune system, destroying white blood cells, and may cause lymphoma (see p.63) or leukaemia. It may also destroy developing red blood cells, causing anaemia (see p.59). Infected cats die within a few years. Vets may carry out blood tests to identify FeLV. Cats at risk of infection can be vaccinated.

FIV

Feline immunodeficiency virus (FIV) is carried in saliva, blood, and other body fluids, and is usually passed on by cat bites (FIV cannot be passed to humans). Once infected, a cat is "FIV-positive" for life. However, it may take months or years for signs of the disease to appear. FIV attacks the immune system, making the cat unable to fight off infections and cancer. Signs include weight loss, lethargy, fever, inflamed mouth and gums, and persistent or recurrent infections. FIV is diagnosed by a blood test. There is no cure, and currently no recommended vaccine, but preventing further infections can help to keep cats healthy.

FIP

The virus that causes feline infectious peritonitis (FIP) is a form of the common feline coronavirus. Cats may catch the virus by swallowing it after contact with infected cats or faeces. Most

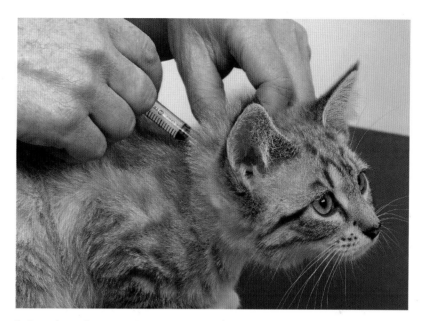

infected cats have no signs or only mild gastroenteritis. However, in rare cases the virus mutates to become FIP, especially in very young or old cats. FIP causes fever, weight loss, appetite loss, and jaundice. There are two main forms. The wet (acute) form causes a bloated abdomen, muffled heart sounds, and difficulty breathing. The dry (chronic) form causes inflammation in blood vessels and body tissues, especially in the eyes and brain. FIP is usually fatal.

Rabies

This viral infection is highly dangerous as it can be passed to humans. Rabies is a global problem; only a few countries, such as the UK, are unaffected. The virus is transmitted in saliva, usually by a bite from an infected animal. Signs may take several weeks to appear. They include irritable or vicious behaviour, paralysis of facial and throat muscles, seizures, and death. Vaccination can prevent the disease. Cats travelling out of or into the UK must meet the requirements of the Pet Travel Scheme.

△ **Vaccinating a cat**
Most vaccines are given by injection under the skin, but certain vaccines may be given as eye or nose drops.

"Vaccination **protects** your cat from **infectious diseases.**"

Vaccination

A vaccine against an infectious organism is formulated to stimulate the immune system so that it is ready to protect the cat if exposed to the actual infection. All cats should be vaccinated against feline panleukopenia, FCV, and FHV. Cats at high risk for FeLV, *Chlamydophila felis*, and rabies may also need vaccination. Kittens have their first vaccinations from 8–9 weeks old (12 weeks for rabies), and should have a full booster vaccination 12 months later (except for rabies). Boarding catteries will require you to leave a fully up-to-date vaccination certificate with your cat when he is admitted.

Reproductive disorders

Most cats are neutered at about 4 months of age, so are unlikely to develop disorders of the reproductive system. However, "intact" toms (males) and queens (females) may develop problems with their reproductive organs.

Signs of a problem

- Distended abdomen (queen)
- Thick, bloody, or foul-smelling discharge from vulva
- Inflamed mammary glands
- Lumps in mammary glands
- Retained testicles

Maturity and mating

Kittens usually reach puberty at around 6 months of age, although females can show signs of being in season, or on heat, as young as 4 months. Queens naturally start coming into season with increasing day length in spring, but indoor cats may have seasons all year round. Seasons may occur every 3 weeks, but queens do not ovulate (release eggs from their ovaries) until they mate. However, this means that matings usually result in pregnancy. If a queen mates with several toms, the kittens in her litter may have more than one father. Queens can naturally produce up to three litters per year.

Female problems

Infertility in queens can occur if problems during mating prevent ovulation from occurring. It may also be due to a hormone imbalance, or an infectious organism such as *Toxoplasma* or possibly *Chlamydophila felis*. A vet may perform blood and urine tests and scans to identify the underlying cause.

Stress or infection may cause a pregnant mother to abort her fetuses or reabsorb them into her body. Giving birth may cause the uterus to be pushed outside the body. This is dangerous and needs immediate veterinary attention. Another serious problem is infection of the uterus, causing a build-up of pus. This may develop a few days after giving birth or in the non-pregnant queen after a succession of seasons. Signs include fever, loss of appetite, and a bloody or pus-filled vaginal discharge. Nursing mothers may develop inflamed teats (mastitis) due to overfilling or infection.

Older queens may develop cysts on the ovaries or tumours of the ovaries, uterus, or mammary glands. A vet may use ultrasound scans and take biopsies to identify these problems, and perform surgery to remove the growths.

Male problems

The problem of male infertility is rare, but one possible cause is retained testicles (cryptorchidism). In a male fetus the testicles develop in the abdomen, and by the time the kitten is born they usually descend and hang under the tail in the scrotum. If both are retained in the abdomen beyond 6 months of age, the tom will be sterile because his body temperature will be too high to allow sperm production. Injury, infections, or testicular cancer can also reduce male fertility.

◁ **Queen in season**
A female in season may call to nearby males, roll around on her back, and crouch with her rump in the air.

Urinary disorders

The urinary system comprises the kidneys, which filter blood and generate urine, and the bladder and urethra, through which urine is expelled. Problems in the urinary system can be serious and need prompt medical attention.

Signs of a problem

- Squatting frequently but passing only a little urine
- Crying when urinating
- Washing under tail excessively
- Frequently passing a lot of urine
- Change in colour of urine from normal pale yellow
- Passing cloudy rather than clear urine
- Urinating outside litter box or in unusual places
- Increased thirst

◁ **Cat licking under tail**
Pain in the urethra, or irritation from urine, may cause cats to lick their genital areas excessively. This can lead to inflammation and hair loss.

△ **Urinary disorders and stress**
Physical or emotional stress may aggravate FLUTD, by increasing muscle activity in the bladder or reducing the cat's resistance to infection.

FLUTD

Feline lower urinary tract disease (FLUTD) is a general term for disorders of the bladder and the urethra. Causes may include stress, stones or crystals in the bladder, bacterial infection leading to bladder inflammation (cystitis), muscle weakness or spasm, blockage in the urethra, and anatomical abnormalities. Cystitis with no identifiable cause is termed "feline idiopathic cystitis". Most cases of FLUTD are idiopathic.

Overweight and inactive middle-aged or older cats are at greater risk of FLUTD. Cats fed on a dry diet, with insufficient access to water, may also develop it. Signs include frequent unsuccessful attempts to urinate, pain when passing urine, dark (bloody) or cloudy urine, and excessive licking of the genitals.

You should contact your vet if your cat is obviously struggling or is in pain. Inability to urinate can lead to kidney failure. The vet will carry out urine tests and may use radiography and ultrasound scans to identify possible causes. Treatment may include tactics and treatments such as pheromone diffusers to reduce stress, surgery to relieve urethral blockage, antibiotics to treat bacterial infection, or a diet to help dissolve stones and crystals.

CKD

Chronic kidney disease (CKD) is the most common disorder in older cats. Gradually the kidneys become less efficient at filtering out waste, causing toxins to build up in the body. Other causes include genetic disease (see also "Polycystic kidney disease" on p.46), infections, tumours, drugs, or poisons. Signs include increased urination, increase in thirst, vomiting, and loss of weight. The cat may also become weak, with a dull coat and bad breath. Treatment may include medication and diet to support kidney function. Vets may offer screening tests to detect early signs of CKD in older cats.

Nursing a sick cat

If your cat is ill, consult your vet and follow any instructions on care and home treatment. There are also some simple things that you can do to make your cat comfortable during recuperation.

Creating a sick room

You will need to keep a sick or injured cat indoors so that you can easily monitor him. Keep your cat confined in a warm, quiet room or even in a wire crate. Provide food and water, and a litter tray in an area away from the food. Make up a warm bed on the floor for easy access; you could use a cardboard box, which can easily be replaced if soiled. Cut one side away, line the base with newspaper, and add cosy blankets and perhaps a hot-water bottle.

Handling your cat

A sick or injured cat may want to hide himself away and try to avoid the extra stress of having medicine or other treatment. Handle your cat gently and in a calm, unhurried, confident way – any anxiety on your part could make him stressed and uncooperative. Your cat may feel comforted if you spend time just talking quietly to him and petting him (if he will accept this), so that he does not associate you solely with treatment.

Home care when ill

A cat may lose interest in food when ill or if his sense of smell is impaired (see cat flu, p.58). Call a vet if your cat has gone for more than a day without eating, especially if he is overweight, as lack of food can harm the liver. Let food come to room temperature, or warm it slightly in the oven, to increase its smell and make it more appetizing. In addition, offer small pieces of strong-smelling, tasty foods. If your cat is struggling to eat properly, you may need to feed him by hand.

If your cat is vomiting or has diarrhoea, offer a teaspoon every hour of bland food such as poached skinned chicken or an appropriate prescription diet. Once the gastric upset ceases, gradually increase portion size and keep your cat on this diet for three or four days, before weaning back to normal meals. Provide cooled, boiled drinking water at all times. Call a vet if a gastric disorder persists.

Your cat may need help with grooming. In particular, clean away discharge from the eyes, keep the nose and mouth clean to help the cat breathe and smell food, and clean under the tail if the cat has diarrhoea. Use a cotton wool ball

△ **Safe space**
A wire crate should be large enough to let the cat walk around. Line it with newspaper, and add food, a water bowl, a bed, and a litter tray.

▷ **Staying indoors**
You will need to keep your cat indoors, in a confined area, for his own safety and so you can easily monitor him and give care.

Giving your cat a tablet

Step 1
With a helper holding the cat, place your hand over the top of the head. Try not to bend the whiskers.

Step 2
Grasp the jaws between forefinger and thumb and gently tip the head back. With the other forefinger, open the mouth.

Step 3
Place the tablet on the back of the tongue. Close the cat's mouth and stroke the throat to make the cat swallow.

moistened in clean, warm water. For itchy skin or minor wounds, bathe the area with saline solution – a teaspoon of salt dissolved in 500ml (1 pint) of warm water. If the cat resists, wrap him in a towel, leaving the sore part exposed.

After an operation
A cat that has had a general anaesthetic may be groggy for a while. Stay with him until he is fully alert. Keep him indoors until any surgical wound has healed and dressings or stitches have been removed. Your vet may fit a soft, cone-shaped collar to prevent your cat worrying at a wound, and you may have to remove this to let the cat eat. For small wounds on the limbs, the vet may cover the area with "anti-lick" strips impregnated with a taste that cats dislike. You should check a dressing or a plaster cast several times a day to ensure it is clean and dry. If the cat seems in pain (hiding, resisting examination, or unwilling to eat), or if the wound looks sore or has a discharge, contact your vet.

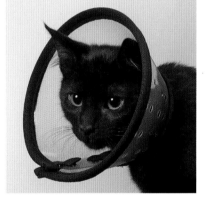

Giving medication
It is essential to follow your vet's directions on giving medication and complete the full course, especially with antibiotics. Ask your vet to demonstrate how to give eye or ear drops or dose the cat with a syringe.

Medications should be given by an adult. Give tablets by hand (see above) to make sure the cat swallows them and that other pets do not take them. It may help to crush tablets into a small amount of tasty food, or wrap a small amount of food around them (do not do this if the tablet has to be taken on an empty stomach).

◁ **Elizabethan collar**
A soft or rigid cone-shaped collar, sometimes called an Elizabethan collar, is designed to stop a cat licking a wound or surgical incision site.

Alternative therapies
Many pet owners have an interest in using alternative therapies to maintain their cat's health or to treat certain disorders, such as allergies and joint pain. Some therapies involve plant-based or other natural remedies, such as herbalism and traditional Chinese medicine. Others involve touch and manipulation, such as TTouch, chiropractic, and shiatsu. Other alternative therapies include acupuncture and magnetic therapy to stimulate the cat's natural healing mechanisms. Some of these therapies may even be covered by your pet's insurance policy. If you do wish to try an alternative therapy, ask your vet for guidance. All practitioners should be registered with a veterinary governing body, such as the Royal College of Veterinary Surgeons (RCVS) in the UK.

Caring for an **elderly cat**

Thanks to improvements in food and health care, cats now often live beyond 12 years of age. Older cats may develop age-related conditions, but with a little extra care your cat can still have a comfortable, happy life.

Home care

You may need to make adaptations to your cat's diet and living conditions as he ages (see pp.28–9). Your vet may recommend a "senior" diet, which will supply the correct nutrients for the changes in your cat's metabolism and digestive processes. Your cat may prefer to eat smaller meals more often during the day. If he seems less interested in eating, try warmer or tastier foods to tempt him. It is also helpful to weigh your cat every 2 weeks; older cats can gain excess weight due to inactivity, or lose weight due to difficulty with eating or conditions such as hyperthyroidism (see p.61).

Your cat may need help with grooming hard-to-reach places, so brushing a few times a week will make him more comfortable. Clip his claws regularly, as they can grow harder with age and become overgrown if he is not very active.

If your cat is becoming less agile, put his food and water bowls and a litter tray on the floor, in quiet places where he won't be disturbed. Use boxes or furniture as "stepping stones" to help your cat reach his favourite perches or windowsills.

Have several warm, comfortable cat beds around your home, in places where your cat already enjoys sleeping. If your cat is having trouble with soiling, use washable beds or cardboard boxes lined with newspaper that can be thrown away.

Even if your cat still prefers to urinate and defecate outdoors, it is wise to have litter trays in the house. Your cat may become less keen on going outdoors, either to avoid other cats or because he no longer has the urge to explore.

Even an old cat still likes to have fun. Playing with your cat helps to keep his mind active and allows him to express his natural instincts, although you will have to play more gently than before.

> **"Let the vet know** if you have **noticed any changes** in your cat's **normal activities."**

◁ **Using stairs**
A cat with arthritis or stiff joints may find it hard to use stairs, so have food, water, beds, and litter trays on each floor of your house.

△ **A cosy bed**
If your elderly cat has a favourite resting place, such as in front of the fire, place a blanket, cushion, or soft cat bed there to help him be more comfortable.

Senior cat clinics

As your cat grows older he will need more frequent health checks. Many veterinary practices now offer clinics for older cats, to detect and deal with age-related health problems.

Your vet will be able to advise you on your cat's ideal body weight, and on diet and nutritional supplements. Let the vet know if you have noticed any changes in your cat's normal activities, as these could signal the start of health problems.

The vet may carry out basic tests such as urine and blood tests, to identify problems such as kidney disease. There are many treatments now available to help manage chronic conditions – even senility. The vet or practice nurse can also help with tasks such as clipping claws.

Warning signs

You will need to keep a closer eye on your cat to detect any alterations in his normal habits. In particular, you should let your vet know if you notice any of the following changes.

Watch for any increase in appetite, with your cat seeming ravenously hungry but losing weight even with regular meals. In contrast, if your cat is obviously hungry but turns away from certain foods (especially hard foods), or paws at his mouth, he may have problems with his teeth or with swallowing.

Increased thirst may cause your cat to use the litter tray more than usual, and start drinking from odd places such as ponds and bath taps. An elderly cat may also become dehydrated. Check by grasping the scruff of the neck and letting go. The skin should fall back instantly; if it does not, the cat may not be getting enough liquid.

Alert your vet if your cat is straining or crying when he passes faeces or urine, or if he starts having "accidents" in the home.

Stiff joints or arthritis can cause difficulty with running and jumping, and your cat may become unable to groom his back and rear end. As he ages, your cat may lose his vision, causing him to bump into things or misjudge heights. A cat that is feeling very ill or showing signs of dementia may become more withdrawn or aggressive, hide away, or miaow more than usual.

◁ **Unusual drinking habits**
Let your vet know if your cat is drinking more water than usual, including from strange places such as ponds, taps, or the bath.

Euthanasia

For a very old or sick cat, sometimes the kindest thing to do is to give him a dignified, peaceful ending. Euthanasia is usually carried out in a veterinary practice, but it can be done at home (you will need to book in advance). The vet will give an injection of anaesthetic – in effect, an overdose – into a front leg vein. The cat will become unconscious before passing away. There may be involuntary movements, and the bladder or bowels may empty. You can ask for your cat to be cremated, or take the body home. You may wish to bury your cat in your garden, another favourite place outdoors, or a pet cemetery.

4

Feline emergencies

Basic first aid

If your cat is injured, carrying out some basic first aid checks may make the difference between life and death. Be prepared for emergencies and follow these guidelines to keep your cat safe until you reach the vet.

Normal vital signs

Temperature	38–39°C (100.5–102.5°F)
Pulse	110–180 beats per minute
Respirations	20–30 per minute
Capillary refill time*	less than two seconds

*time for gum to regain pink colour after being blanched by gentle pressure with finger

▽ **Alerting your vet**
If your cat has a serious injury or a sudden, severe illness, call the vet immediately so the staff will be ready when you bring the cat in.

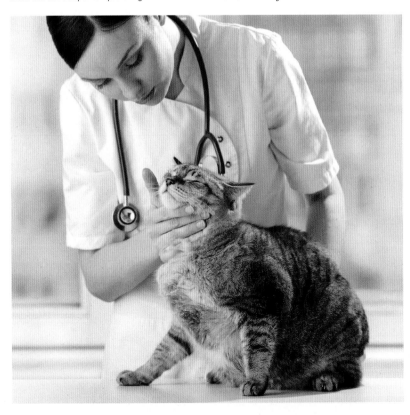

Danger signs

Keep the telephone numbers for your vet and the emergency vet service where you can easily find them. Call a vet immediately if your cat has any of the following signs.

■ Loss of consciousness
■ Seizures
■ Rapid breathing, panting, or struggling for breath
■ Fast or weak pulse
■ Hot or cold temperature – feel the ears and pads of the paws
■ Pale gums
■ Limping, difficulty in walking, or paralysis
■ Difficulty in standing, or collapse
■ Serious injuries

Handling an injured cat

Check the cat for broken bones and open wounds or bleeding, but try not to move him. Take care – even the most loving pet may bite or lash out if it is in severe pain.

If the cat has a fracture or severe wound, lay him on a blanket with the injury uppermost and wrap the wound up gently. Do not try to splint broken bones yourself.

If your cat has a haemorrhage (severe bleeding), raise the bleeding area above the level of the cat's heart, if possible, and apply direct pressure with a pad of cloth, to stem the blood flow.

Lift the cat carefully, with one hand under the shoulders and the other under the hips, and place him in a carrier.

Loss of consciousness

If the cat is lying motionless, check for consciousness. Touch the corner of the eye to see if it blinks; flick the tip of the ear to see if the ear twitches; or pinch the skin between the toes to see if the cat flinches.

If the cat is unconscious, check "ABC" – airway, breathing, and circulation.

■ Airway – open the mouth and pull the tongue forwards. Gently sweep your little finger over the

> " ...check the "ABCs" – **airway**, **breathing**, and **circulation**."

First aid kit

A first aid kit for your cat will enable you to deal with minor injuries yourself or, in emergencies, provide care until you can reach a vet. Some pet shops sell veterinary-approved kits, or you can make up your own using the articles shown here. Keep the kit easily accessible at all times.

Adhesive bandage

Disposable gloves

Thermometer

Tweezers

First aid box

Saline wash

Bandage

Cotton wool

Scissors

back of the tongue to check for anything blocking the throat.

■ Breathing – look for chest movements and feel for breath from the nostrils.

■ Circulation – feel the chest for the heart beat, and the inside of the back leg, near the top, for the pulse.

If there is no breathing or pulse, give heart massage by squeezing the chest under the forelegs with one hand, at two compressions per second. Every 10 compressions, give a "breath" — press the chest with both hands, or cup your hands around the face and blow into the nose. Continue for up to 10 minutes or until the cat starts breathing.

Shock

Shock is a life-threatening loss of circulation caused by severe injury or heavy internal bleeding, poisoning, or a severe allergic reaction. The cat will feel cold to the touch, breathing and pulse will be weak and rapid, and the gums will be very pale. Wrap the cat in blankets to preserve body heat, but do not constrict the chest. If he is having problems breathing, lay him on his side with the head tilted downwards. Monitor ABC.

Hypothermia

Abnormally low body temperature can develop if a cat spends too long outside in cold weather or falls into freezing water. Bring the cat into a warm room and wrap him in warm, dry blankets – warm the blankets first in a tumble dryer. The cat will need urgent veterinary attention.

Heat stroke

A cat can easily develop heat stroke on a hot day if he is shut in a room or a vehicle with no access to water. The cat may be panting and distressed, with red gums. This needs urgent action; heat stroke may quickly progress to collapse, coma, and death. Lower the body temperature by placing the cat in a cool room with a fan, or placing cool, damp towels on the body, especially around the armpits and groin.

Drowning

If you can reach a drowning cat, pull him to safety and dry with a towel. If he is not moving, hold him by the hind legs, with his body hanging down, then shake him up and down to clear water from the lungs. If he is not breathing, try resuscitation.

Road traffic accidents

Road accidents are the main cause of serious injury and death in cats. Minimize risks by keeping your cat indoors at busy times and at night, and have your cat neutered – neutered cats are less likely to stray and get into danger. Sadly, many road accident victims do not survive. If you find a body, check it for a collar and take it to a local vet to be scanned for a microchip. If the cat is alive, move him only if he is in danger of being hit by another vehicle, or if you feel that moving him will not worsen any injury.

△ **Risk of heat stroke**
A conservatory or a room with big windows can get very hot in direct sunlight. A cat trapped in a room like this will be at risk of heat stroke.

Wounds and burns

Many skin wounds can be treated at home, although you will need to discuss them with your vet if there are complications. Burns are an emergency and need immediate veterinary care.

Minor wounds

Small cuts and grazes can be treated at home. Look for bleeding, moist fur, or a scab, or the cat licking an area intensely. Gently wipe away blood and dirt using a cotton wool ball moistened in saline solution – a teaspoon of salt stirred into 500ml (1 pint) of clean, warm water. Cut away hair around the wound using blunt-ended scissors.

Small skin wounds can sometimes occur with more extensive internal damage. Check for heat, swelling, or discoloured skin around the wound, and watch for signs of pain or shock (see p.75). Small wounds can also become infected, so look for signs of abscess formation, such as swelling and pus.

More serious wounds

Wounds that are bleeding profusely need prompt veterinary attention, as do bites and scratches from other animals (as these could become infected). Eye injuries also need urgent care.

Call the vet before setting out. To stop bleeding, press on the wound with a gauze pad or clean cloth soaked in clean, cold water. If the bleeding does not stop after two minutes, cover the wound with a clean, dry pad (or cloth) and bandage in place. For an eye wound, cover the eye with a gauze pad and tape in place. For very heavy bleeding or a severe wound, apply first aid (see pp.74–5).

Burns

Cats may suffer burns from fires, hot surfaces, scalding liquids, electrical appliances, or chemicals. These injuries can be very serious, with damage to deep tissues, and need urgent veterinary attention.

For a burn or scald, remove the cat from the heat source without endangering yourself. Flood the affected area with clean, cold water for at least 10 minutes, then cover it with a moist sterile dressing. Keep the cat warm during the journey to the vet.

If your cat has been electrocuted (for example, by chewing through a power cord), turn off the power first, or use a wooden broom handle to move the power source away from the cat. Carry out first aid (see pp.74–5) and take the cat to the vet immediately.

For chemical burns, call the vet at once and say which chemical is responsible. If the vet advises rinsing, put on rubber gloves to avoid contaminating yourself, and flush the area carefully with water.

◁ **Protective wrap**
A bandage will protect a wound until a vet can treat it. Make sure the bandage is not too tight; the skin around it should feel warm.

Stings and bites

Cats are naturally inquisitive, and occasionally their curiosity about other creatures can lead them into trouble. If your cat incurs an insect sting or venomous bite the treatment will depend on the culprit.

Bee or wasp stings

If your cat has been stung, move him away from any other bees or wasps to avoid further stings. Call the vet for advice, and take the cat in if he develops breathing difficulties or becomes unsteady on his feet. If your cat goes into shock (see p.75), take him to the vet immediately.

Otherwise, try to remove a bee sting with tweezers as soon as possible. Grasp it where it meets the cat's skin and take care not to grasp the tiny sac at the top, or you might squeeze out more venom. For a bee sting, bathe the area with bicarbonate of soda mixed in warm water. A wasp sting should be bathed with vinegar diluted in water. Apply an ice pack (such as a bag of frozen peas wrapped in a cloth) to reduce inflammation.

Mosquito and gnat bites

Most cats will suffer only minor irritation from small biting insects, such as mosquitoes and gnats. However, there are some cats that may suffer a severe allergic reaction (see p.75) to mosquitoes. If your cat is hypersensitive to mosquito bites, it is best to prevent exposure to these flying insects by keeping the cat indoors at dawn and dusk.

Venomous animals

Cats may be bitten by other cats (see pp.50–1), but bites from venomous animals can be more serious. Dangers from snakes, toads, scorpions, and spiders vary

△ **Inquisitive hunter**
Cats often enjoy hunting insects, snakes, and other small animals in play, but venomous or toxic animals can cause pain and sometimes serious physical effects.

between countries. In the UK, the adder is the only native venomous snake (although captive exotic reptiles can also be a hazard).

Adder bites are rare, but can cause serious swelling, nausea, vomiting, and dizziness; your cat may lick the area, and you may see two puncture wounds in the skin.

Some toad species secrete toxins onto their skin, which can cause inflammation in a cat's mouth and perhaps retching.

If your cat has been affected, call the vet immediately and say what kind of animal was involved (or take a photo if you can) so that the vet can obtain the correct anti-venom. You need to take the cat to the veterinary surgery as soon as you can.

Choking and poisoning

Cats explore their world by sniffing and tasting, pouncing and chewing. Although they are discerning, their inquisitiveness puts them at risk of swallowing dangerous items or poisonous substances.

Choking

Cats can choke on a variety of objects. Some objects, such as bird bones, may get wedged in the mouth; others, such as pebbles, may block the throat (airway). Items such as tinsel, ribbon, string, or thread can get tangled around the tongue or, if swallowed, cause problems in the intestines.

A choking cat will cough, drool, and gag, and paw frantically at its mouth. If the airway is blocked, the cat will struggle to breathe and may lose consciousness.

Call the vet and take the cat in. First, wrap the cat in a towel. Hold the top of the head with one hand, and open the lower jaw with the other. Look inside the mouth. If the object is easy to dislodge, try to remove it quickly with tweezers.

If an object is blocking the airway, use the Heimlich manoeuvre. Lay the cat on its side with its head lower than its body. Place one hand on the back and the other on the belly, just below the ribs. Give four sharp pushes up and in, towards the ribs. Check the mouth again, and remove any debris with one finger. If the cat has stopped breathing, give artificial respiration (see p.75).

Poisoning

Cats may ingest poisons from prey animals, toxic plants, household chemicals, medicines, or even some human foods. If you think your cat has been poisoned, even if he is showing no signs, contact your vet. If you see any signs of poisoning, take the cat to the vet, together with a sample of what he has swallowed. If a cat has a toxic substance on his coat or paws, wrap the cat in a towel so he cannot lick off any more of the substance.

Dangerous chemicals

Some common chemicals can be lethal for cats. Keep these out of reach of your cat (see pp.16–17).

■ Antifreeze (ethylene glycol) – make sure your car does not leak antifreeze and ensure that any containers are stored safely. For a cat, even a tiny amount can cause kidney damage, unsteadiness, seizures, coma, and death.

■ Household cleaners – bleaches, detergents, fabric softeners, and similar chemicals can irritate the cat's mouth and burn the throat.

■ Paints and solvents – cats can swallow paint when licking it off themselves, or breathe in dangerous fumes from paints and solvents. Never let a cat near wet paint or open paint cans. Ensure that you ventilate rooms during and after using paints and solvents.

Poisonous plants

Many household and garden plants can be toxic to cats, either when eaten or when the cat brushes against the plant and then licks himself. Some common examples are given below; ask your vet for a more complete list.

■ *Cordyline* (common garden plant for foliage) and *Dracaena* (houseplant) – both of these plants can cause liver or kidney damage.

Household clutter
Cats may swallow foreign objects both in the home and outdoors. Do not leave items such as plants with thorns or sharp needles, small toys, or string where a cat can eat them.

▽ **Outdoor dangers**
Some cats are tempted to chew house or garden plants. To minimize risks, make sure to move or get rid of any plants that might be toxic.

▷ **Paint hazard**
Cats can easily get wet paint on themselves if they walk through it or rub up against it, or if they explore open paint cans.

■ Lilies – all parts (including the pollen) are toxic to cats, damaging the kidneys.

■ Spider plants – although not highly toxic, the bitter taste causes salivation, vomiting, and lethargy.

Medicines and foods

Medicines and, surprisingly, some of our food can sometimes be harmful for cats.

■ Human medicines are an obvious hazard. Paracetamol is especially dangerous – even one tablet can be fatally toxic to a cat.

■ Dog medicines can be toxic to cats. In addition, never give medicine prescribed for one cat to another, as it may be harmful for that cat.

■ "Spot-on" flea treatments can be toxic if swallowed, so apply them to the back of the cat's neck, where the cat cannot reach while grooming himself.

■ Dangerous human foods include alcoholic or caffeinated drinks, chocolate, garlic, grapes and raisins, and onions. Do not let your cat eat these or walk on tables or worktops while you are preparing food.

Bait for vermin

Rat and mouse poisons, and slug baits, are designed to kill pests but can also be lethal for cats. These poisons can attack the cat's nervous system, causing muscle tremors, unsteadiness, collapse, and seizures. Some rat or mouse poisons can also cause internal bleeding. Your cat may be at risk if he eats the poison directly or if he eats a poisoned prey animal. If your cat has swallowed vermin bait, call the vet and take the cat in immediately, together with the packet of bait (or the remains of any prey animals). The vet will make your cat vomit to expel the poison, and may give an antidote if possible. Never try to make your cat vomit yourself.

"If a cat has a **toxic substance** on his coat or paws, **wrap** the cat **in a towel** so it **cannot lick off** any more of the substance."

5

Breeding

Breeding and pregnancy

The idea of your cat surrounded by cute kittens may be appealing, but breeding is a serious commitment. As well as providing extra care for the mother, you will have to plan ahead for the kittens' future.

Planned breeding

Do not consider breeding from your cat unless you have good reason to believe that you will be able to find a home for every kitten. Many kittens end up in rescue shelters or are put down because they are unwanted. If you own a pedigree cat of a popular breed you may find a ready demand for her kittens, although you should never be motivated by profit (and the expenses involved in breeding can be considerable). Should you decide to let your pedigree have a litter, you will need to do some research to find a reputable breeder with a suitable stud tom.

Mating

Unneutered cats are considered mature enough for planned breeding by about 12 months of age, although they can become sexually active before then.

The females, known as "queens", come into season in cycles of 14–21 days, mainly during spring and summer, with each season lasting for three or four days. When a queen is ready to mate, or "in heat", she will show obvious signs, including constant calling, lying down with her rump raised, and rolling or rubbing herself against the floor. The scent of her urine will also attract any toms in the area.

This is the time to take the queen to the breeder, where she and the stud tom you have chosen will be placed in adjacent pens. When she starts making advances to her prospective mate, the two cats will be allowed access to one another. Mating usually occurs several times, so it is common practice to leave the pair together for at least a day or two. Once home, keep the queen confined to the house for

several days. She could still be in heat and attractive to non-pedigree local toms.

Signs of pregnancy

The average length of pregnancy in cats is between 63 and 68 days. The first sign that mating has been successful will be a slight reddening of your cat's nipples, which appears around the third week of pregnancy. In the following weeks, the queen will steadily gain weight and her shape will change as her belly swells. The kittens she is carrying can be easily felt during a vet's examination after about the fifth week. Never try to carry out any kind of investigation yourself. Unskilled handling of a

▽ **Expecting**
A pregnant queen will become a little less agile as she grows larger, but if she is in good health she will still enjoy her usual activities.

△ **A suitable mate**
When choosing a pedigree mate for your cat, find out about the stud cat's health and ancestry. A reputable breeder should be prepared to answer any questions.

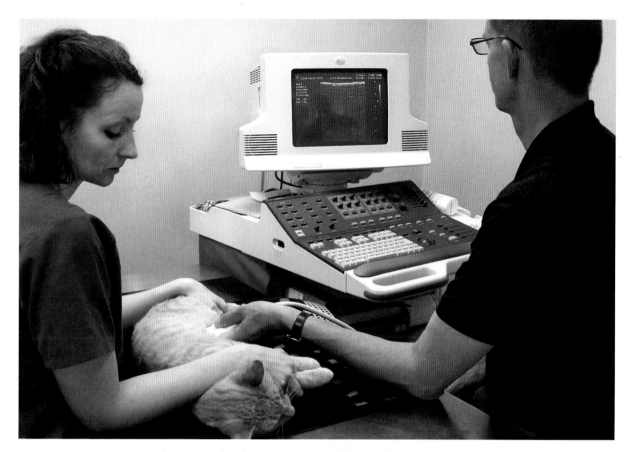

pregnant queen can cause damage to both the mother and her developing kittens.

Prenatal care

An expectant cat needs plenty of nourishment and her appetite will increase towards the end of her pregnancy. Your vet can give you guidance on feeding, and will suggest suitable supplements to add to your cat's diet if necessary. It is also vital to have your cat checked for parasites, as she could pass these on to her kittens. The vet may ask you to bring a sample of your cat's stools to test for intestinal worms, and can also give you advice on which flea treatments are safe to use during pregnancy.

Well before your cat is due to give birth, prepare a kittening box for her in a quiet corner. This can be bought ready-made, but a sturdy cardboard box serves just as well. It should be open at one side to give the queen easy access, but not so low that new-born kittens can roll out. A thick lining of newspaper provides warmth and comfort, and is easily replaced when soiled. Encourage the queen to spend time in the box so that she feels at home in her kittening area and, hopefully, will go there when labour begins (see pp.84–5).

If your cat is naturally active, there is no need to stop her from jumping or climbing, but she should not be allowed outdoors during the last two weeks of pregnancy. Avoid picking her up unless absolutely necessary, and ensure that children handle her gently when they play with her.

△ **Ultrasound scan**
The vet may use an ultrasound scanner to confirm whether your cat is pregnant. The developing kittens can be seen on an ultrasound scan within 3–4 weeks of pregnancy.

Unplanned pregnancy

Accidents happen – perhaps because neutering (see p.89) is delayed or a queen destined for a pedigree mate escapes vigilance for a few crucial hours. Ask your vet for advice as soon as you suspect your cat is pregnant. Pregnancy could compromise your cat's health, especially if she is not fully mature. If a queen mates with more than one tom during the same heat cycle, the kittens may have different fathers. Your vet can help with advice on re-homing accidental litters.

Queening and postnatal care

Producing kittens – queening – is something most cats experience without difficulty. Your role is simply to keep a close watch while staying as unobtrusive as possible. Always contact a vet if problems arise.

Checklist

■ Telephone number of veterinary practice
■ Clean towels
■ Newspaper
■ Rubbish bags
■ Latex gloves
■ Disinfectant that is safe for use with cats

Giving birth

When the time for giving birth to her kittens is near, a queen usually becomes restless and may ignore all offers of food. Once her contractions begin, she will probably head for the security of her kittening box. However, queens sometimes change their minds at the last minute as to where they want to give birth, so make sure your cat cannot take herself off to a hidden corner.

During the first stage of labour, which can last up to 6 hours, regular contractions gradually open the cervix (neck of the uterus). The queen will pant and perhaps purr, but she should not seem unduly distressed. A clear vaginal discharge often appears.

As the queen enters the second stage of labour, she begins to strain, or "bear down", with each contraction to push a kitten through the birth canal. Within about 30 minutes, a greyish bubble – which is the membrane that encases the kitten in the uterus – appears at the vaginal opening. A few further contractions propel the kitten out into the world. The final stage of labour expels the placenta (afterbirth); there will be a separate placenta for each kitten.

The rest of the kittens will be born at varying intervals. They may arrive within minutes of each other, although at some births there can be a time lag of an hour or two between deliveries.

With a normal labour and birth, you only need to monitor the situation, without interfering or disturbing the queen by hovering over her too closely. It is necessary to take action if the second stage of labour continues for more than about 2 hours without producing any kittens; there is an abnormally long interval between each delivery; contractions cease but you suspect that not all the kittens are born; or a kitten becomes stuck in the birth canal. Never try to resolve birthing problems yourself. If the queen appears to be in difficulties, ring the vet immediately to ask for advice.

After the birth

In most cases, the queen, even if it is her first litter, knows what to do and wastes no time in dealing with each kitten in turn. She will lick the kitten all over, to remove the birth fluids and surrounding membrane and to stimulate breathing. She will also bite through the umbilical cord that

First wash
As soon as a kitten is born, the mother licks it clean, using her tongue vigorously to remove the surrounding membrane and stimulate the kitten's breathing.

△ **Contented family**
A mother cat relaxes as she suckles her litter. Her first milk, a nutritious fluid called colostrum, contains antibodies to provide the kittens with protection against disease.

attaches the kitten to the placenta. It is quite natural for the mother to eat the placenta, so do not attempt to stop her. Newly washed, the kitten will at once start blindly nosing at its mother in search of a teat to latch on to for its first feed.

If all has gone well, it should not be long before the entire litter and their mother are contentedly bonding with each other. Disturbing them as little as possible, remove soiled bedding from the kittening box and replace it with clean materials. After providing the queen with food, water, and a litter tray

within easy reach so she does not have to move far from her kittens, leave the new family to settle down in peace.

Postnatal complications are unusual in cats, but in the days following delivery you should keep a careful watch on both mother and kittens. In a newly delivered queen, some light vaginal bleeding and discharge is normal and will continue for several days. If you notice any of the following signs in the queen, you must contact your vet immediately:

■ Prolonged or heavy vaginal bleeding, or a foul-smelling, coloured discharge.
■ Heat and swelling around the teats, which may be accompanied by a discharge.
■ Restlessness and loss of appetite.

△ **Dropper feeding**
Rarely, a kitten needs to be hand-reared and fed artificially. It is vital to use the correct equipment, milk formula, and technique, so always ask your vet for advice.

■ Lethargy and lack of interest in her kittens.

Failure to thrive in kittens can also be an indication that the health of the queen needs prompt investigation. Kittens that have been orphaned or rejected by their mother may survive with careful hand-rearing, but it takes time, dedication, and the help of your vet to achieve success.

"With a **normal labour and birth,** you should not need to do anything but **monitor the situation, without disturbing** the queen."

Early kitten care

Looking after the welfare and safety of a new litter of kittens is a big responsibility, but you will not have to take on the task single-handed. Mother cats know instinctively how to raise a family.

The first weeks

Until they have been weaned (see opposite), kittens need to stay with their mother and siblings all the time. The mother cat is not only a protector and source of nutrition, but a teacher of feline behaviour as well. It is through interaction with brothers and sisters that kittens practise their social and life skills. No kitten should be removed from this family support group unless absolutely necessary.

Kittens start playing games together as early as 4 weeks of age and will benefit from a few toys to stimulate their interest. Objects that roll about are always popular, but don't offer anything that could snag and damage tiny claws. Games often turn into rough and tumble, but even if the entire litter becomes a tussling furball there is no need to separate them. They are highly unlikely to do each other harm and this mock fighting is an important part of their mental and physical development.

Keep a constant eye on the whereabouts of young kittens, especially once they are mobile and can climb out of the kittening box. They will wander everywhere and can all too easily end up being trodden on or getting themselves injured while moving around the house. Do not allow them to go outdoors until they have been fully vaccinated (see also Making the home safe, pp.16–7).

Using a litter tray

You will probably find that you have very little work to do in training kittens to use a litter tray. As soon as they find their feet, at around 3 weeks of age, they will start copying their mother and

Stages of development

New-born kittens are blind, deaf, and completely dependent on their mother, but they develop rapidly. Within a few weeks helpless infants turn into lively individuals that have learned all the basic lessons about being a cat. Adulthood is generally reached at around 12 months, although some cats take longer to complete their full growth.

△ **Five days**
The kitten has some sense of the surrounding world, even though the eyes are not yet open. The ears lie flat against the head and hearing is still undeveloped.

△ **Two weeks**
The eyes are now open although vision is imperfect. For a few weeks, all kittens have blue eyes that gradually change to the permanent colour.

△ **Four weeks**
Up and running, tail held erect as a balancing pole, the kitten starts exploring. Sight and hearing are well developed and the digestive system can cope with solid food.

▷ **Eight weeks**
Very active and fascinated by anything and everything, the kitten is instinctively adopting characteristic feline habits such as self-grooming and will practise hunting by pouncing on toys or siblings. Weaning should be fully completed around this stage.

△ **Ten weeks**
Not quite a cat – but almost – the kitten will soon be ready to leave home. It is important for vaccinations to be given at this age.

> "Keep a **constant eye** on the **whereabouts of young kittens**... They will **wander everywhere.**"

◁ **Waiting for adoption**
It is hard to part with kittens you have tended since birth, but these young siblings are already developing into independent characters and are ready for new homes.

head for the tray when she does. Although older cats prefer privacy when they use a litter tray, young kittens often all pile into it together. Provide them with a tray that is large enough for sharing, with shallow sides that they can climb over easily. Kittens have a built-in instinct to scratch around in loose, soft materials and scattered litter is inevitable, so surround the tray with newspaper to catch spillages.

There are bound to be a few accidents, but you can keep these to a minimum by watching kittens for warning signs. If you see a kitten going into a squat, scoop him up gently and put him in the tray. Never make an abrupt grab, or clap your hands in an attempt to stop him urinating or defecating

on the carpet – you will just frighten him. If there is no time to reach the litter tray, lift him on to a sheet of newspaper. When he has finished, put the kitten and paper in the tray for a few moments to reinforce the idea.

Weaning

By about 4 weeks of age, kittens have acquired some of their baby teeth and are ready for weaning – making the change from mother's milk to solid food. As with litter-

tray training, a mother cat can usually be relied upon to demonstrate the skill. The kittens will imitate the way she feeds from her bowl and, apart from providing the meals (see also Monitoring feeding levels, pp.28–9), you should not interfere. Only very occasionally – for example, when a kitten has been orphaned – is hand-weaning necessary. If you face this problem, you should ask your vet for advice.

At the start of weaning, young kittens are more inclined to dabble their feet in the food than to eat it, so place bowls on newspaper and be prepared for messy mealtimes. As their intake of solids increases, kittens become less and less dependent on their mother for nutrition and the mother's milk will gradually dry up. Most kittens are fully weaned at 8 weeks old.

▷ **Learning clean habits**
Kittens grasp the idea of using a litter tray at a very early age. They usually just follow the mother cat's example.

Kitten health checks

For the best possible start, take your kitten to a vet as soon as possible for a comprehensive check-up and protective vaccinations. Follow this with annual health checks throughout your pet's life.

Preparing to visit the vet

Taking your kitten for his first visit to the vet should not be stressful, provided you have prepared him beforehand for the trip. The most important thing to do is accustom the kitten to going in his carrier (see pp.18–19). Practise lifting him in and out, using toys and titbits for encouragement, so that he learns to associate the carrier with treats and feels safe and comfortable when he is in it. Pick up the carrier with the kitten inside and walk around with it so that he becomes used to the sensation of moving. Keep these practice sessions short, and never simply shut a kitten in a carrier and leave him on his own.

If you introduce your kitten to as many people as possible, and other pets if you have them, he is more likely to act calmly when he meets strangers at the veterinary practice. You will be able to stay with your kitten throughout the visit to provide reassurance if he needs it.

First health check

Even if your new kitten has already been vaccinated, an early health check is still important. At the initial appointment the vet will give your kitten a thorough examination. It includes checking eyes and ears, feeling over the entire body for abnormalities, listening to the

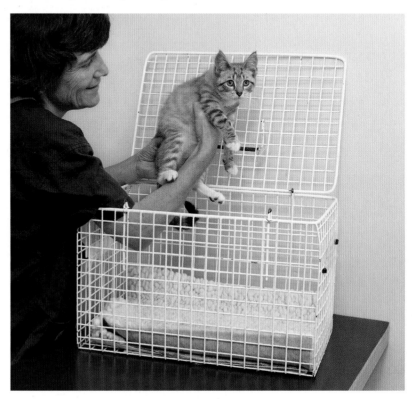

heart, checking the limbs for mobility, and combing through the coat for fleas. If your kitten has not been vaccinated then he will be given his first vaccination, if he is old enough. He will need to return for a second vaccination to complete the course.

At this visit the vet will answer your immediate questions on general cat care and offer valuable advice on the control of common parasites such as worms, fleas,

△ **No surprises**
Prepare for a trauma-free first visit to the vet by teaching your kitten to enjoy going in his carrier.

and ear mites. Now is also the right time to ask the vet about neutering (see right).

Most kittens will come through their first trip to the vet with a clean bill of health, but health issues inevitably arise over the years. Rather than waiting until things go wrong, book your pet an annual veterinary check so that potential problems can be identified and dealt with early on. Follow-up visits include an all-over examination and booster vaccinations if necessary. At these

> "At the **initial appointment** the vet **will give** your kitten a **thorough examination.**"

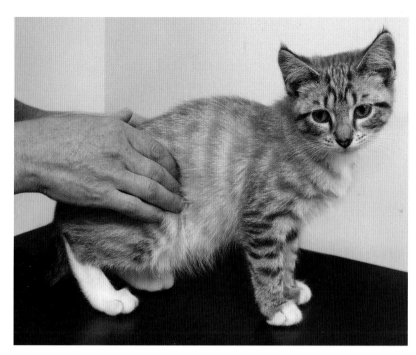

▽ **Combing for fleas**
Your vet will comb through the kitten's coat to pick up fleas or flea dirts. Severe flea infestation can lead to anaemia.

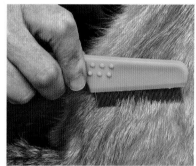

regular checks your vet can draw your attention to any changes that need monitoring, such as an increase or decrease in your cat's weight (see also Monitoring your cat's health, pp.44–5).

Neutering

One of the first things to discuss with your vet is neutering, a routine procedure under general anaesthesia to remove the ovaries and uterus in females and the testicles in males. Apart from preventing unwanted litters, having your kitten neutered has other benefits.

Unneutered male cats often roam far from home in search of a mate and also have the habit of spraying urine around their territory, sometimes even in the house, as a calling card to females. These roving toms can be very aggressive, ready to fight with any cat they see as a rival. Unneutered females are at risk of frequent pregnancies, and when in season they become

agitated, calling constantly to attract males, which is stressful for cats and owners alike. After neutering, these sexual behaviours either disappear or never develop, and both male and female cats are more likely to opt for a peaceful home life. Neutering also reduces the chances of sexually transmitted infections – including a feline version of HIV – being passed between cats, and removes the risk of cancer of the reproductive organs.

Vets usually recommend that kittens be neutered at around 4 months of age, before they reach sexual maturity. Your kitten will stay at the vet for only a few hours and will usually recover from the operation within a few days. A female kitten may have a few sutures in the skin, or none at all. The vet will tell you whether any skin sutures are dissolvable – in which case they should gradually disappear – or whether they need to be removed, usually about 10 days after the operation.

Microchipping

Having your kitten microchipped means that he can be easily identified if he strays or is involved in an accident. A microchip holds a unique number that is kept on a database and can be read by a scanner. Once in place, it is there for life. The vet will insert the tiny device, which is the size of a rice grain, by injecting it under the skin between the shoulder blades. At later visits, your vet can check with a microchip reader that it is in place and working. A microchip is only useful if the contact information stored is kept up-to-date.

Glossary

ANAESTHETIC
A drug used to stop a cat from feeling pain during an operation. A general anaesthetic, usually given as a gas or injection, renders a cat temporarily unconscious. A local anaesthetic numbs a small area of the body.

ANTIBIOTIC
A medicine that destroys or inhibits the growth of microorganisms.

ANTIHISTAMINE
A medicine used to relieve the symptoms of allergy, such as itching or sneezing.

BREED
A group of cats that shares specific aspects of appearance and behaviour passed on from one generation to the next.

CONGENITAL DEFECT
A physical defect that is present from birth; it may be inherited (see Inherited disorder), or it may have arisen in the fetus while it was in the womb.

CORTICOSTEROID
A drug used to relieve inflammation, joint pain, or allergic symptoms such as itching.

CT SCAN
Short for "computed tomography scan". An imaging process that uses computer-processed radiographs to enable bone, soft tissue, and blood vessels to be visualized in slices.

DNA
A protein contained in the cells of every organism, which contains the "instructions" for the development, structure, and function of that organism. DNA is passed on from one generation to the next.

ECG
Short for "electrocardiography", a diagnostic test in which an instrument is used to record the electrical activity in the heart. ECG is used to detect problems such as an abnormal heart rhythm.

ELIZABETHAN COLLAR
A large, cone-shaped plastic collar that is fitted around a cat's neck and head. It is designed to stop a cat licking or biting wounds on its body, and is used to protect an injured area or operation site.

FCV
Feline calicivirus is a major cause of cat flu (see also FHV). A cat can be vaccinated against FCV.

FHV
Feline herpesvirus, one of the two common causes of cat flu (see also FCV). A vaccine is available.

GENE
A section of DNA containing the instructions for producing a particular physical structure or function.

HYPOALLERGENIC DIET
A restricted diet used to identify and control food allergies. Some pet food manufacturers produce special hypoallergenic foods for cats.

INFLAMMATION
A reddening and swelling of a part of the body that can often also be painful. May be caused by infection or injury.

INHERITED DISORDER
Also called a genetic disorder, a health problem that is passed from one generation to the next.

MOGGY
A random-bred cat, often of unknown parentage; often defined as "domestic shorthair" or "domestic longhair".

MRI
Short for "magnetic resonance imaging", a medical scanning technique in which magnetic fields and radio waves are used to produce an image of internal body tissues.

MUTATION
A physical characteristic caused by a defective gene. One such mutation is polydactyly – having extra toes. Some mutations may be preserved deliberately by selective breeding, such as a stumpy tail in the Japanese Bobtail.

NEUTERING
The removal of a cat's reproductive organs so it cannot produce kittens. In males it involves castration (removal of the testicles), and in females it involves spaying (removal of the uterus and ovaries). Non-neutered cats are referred to as "intact".

PEDIGREE
For a cat of a particular breed, the pedigree is a written record of that cat's recent ancestry. A pure-bred cat is sometimes referred to as a "pedigree" cat.

POSTNATAL
A term meaning "following birth": for example, postnatal care of a queen and her kittens.

PRENATAL
A term meaning "before birth": for example, prenatal care of a pregnant queen.

QUEEN
A female cat. The process of giving birth is known as "queening".

RADIOGRAPHY
An imaging process that uses a plate or film that is sensitive to X-rays, gamma rays, or another form of radiation. Radiography is commonly used in medical examinations.

SLICKER BRUSH
A brush with a wide, flat head and thin metal bristles, designed to remove dead, matted hair.

SOCIALIZATION
The process of teaching your kitten to get used to new people and other animals.

TICKED
A coat pattern in which each hair shaft has alternate bands of pale and darker colours; also known as agouti.

TOM
An unneutered male cat.

TOPCOAT
The outer layer of a double coat, consisting of long, tough, weather-resistant hairs.

ULTRASOUND
An image, produced using ultrasonic sound waves, which shows internal tissues. Primarily used by vets for diagnosis and to monitor a pregnancy.

UNDERCOAT
The inner layer of a double coat, consisting of soft, warm, dense hairs.

VACCINATION
Also called immunization, a procedure used to prevent a cat from catching specific bacterial or viral infections. It involves inoculation – injecting a vaccine (a substance containing weakened or dead bacteria or viruses) into a cat. The cat's immune system attacks the organisms in the vaccine, and in so doing will "learn" to attack the actual disease organisms in the future.

WEANING
The process by which kittens graduate from drinking their mother's milk to eating solid food. It naturally happens between 4 and 8 weeks of age.

Useful contacts

UK

SOURCES OF NEW CATS AND KITTENS

Reputable rescue organizations are a good source for new kittens and adult cats. Try to find a centre where they make the effort to assess all the cats in their care so you can choose one with a temperament to suit your lifestyle. The following are useful organizations to contact when looking for a new cat:

Battersea Dogs and Cats Home

www.battersea.org.uk
Email: info@battersea.org.uk
Tel: 020 7622 3626
4 Battersea Park Road, London, SW8 4AA

Blue Cross

www.bluecross.org.uk
Tel: 0300 777 1897
Shilton Road, Burford, Oxon, OX18 4PF

Cat's Protection League

www.cats.org.uk
Tel: 08707 708 649
National Cat Centre, Chelwood Gate, Haywards Heath, West Sussex RH17 7TT

Royal Society for the Prevention of Cruelty to Animals

www.rspca.org.uk
Tel: 0300 1234 555
RSPCA Enquiries Service, Wilberforce Way, Southwater, Horsham, West Sussex RH13 9RS

Wood Green Animal Shelters

www.woodgreen.org.uk
Tel: 0844 248 8181
Wood Green, The Animals Charity, King's Bush Farm, London Road, Godmanchester, Cambridgeshire PE29 2NH

BEHAVIOURAL PROBLEMS

If your cat has behavioural problems, it is best to get help fast. Look for someone with both practical experience and academic knowledge. They should be registered with the Association of Pet Behaviour Counsellors or APBC (see below), work on veterinary referral, and be insured.

Association of Pet Behaviour Counsellors

www.apbc.org.uk
Email: info@apbc.org.uk
Tel: 01386 751151
PO Box 46, Worcester, WR8 9YS

OTHER INFORMATION

The Governing Council of the Cat Fancy is a registration body for the breeding and showing of pure-bred cats, and also offers advice on buying and breeding pedigrees. International Cat Care (formerly known as the Feline Advisory Bureau) provides a wealth of information on caring for cats.

Governing Council of the Cat Fancy

www.gccfcats.org
Tel: 01278 427 575
5 King's Castle Business Park, The Drove, Bridgwater, Somerset TA6 4AG

International Cat Care

www.icatcare.org
Email: info@icatcare.org
Tel: 01747 781 782
Taeselbury High Street, Tisbury, Wiltshire SP3 6LD

USA and CANADA

SOURCES OF NEW CATS AND KITTENS

Reputable rescue organizations are a good source for new kittens and adult cats. Try to find a centre where they make the effort to assess all the cats in their care so you can choose one with a temperament to suit your lifestyle. The following are useful national organizations to contact when looking for a new cat, though there are many more regional institutions across the US and Canada:

American Society for the Prevention of Cruelty to Animals (ASPCA)

www.aspca.org
Tel: 212-876-7700
424 E. 92nd St, New York, NY 10128-6804

Canadian Federation of Humane Societies

www.cfhs.ca
Email: info@cfhs.ca
Tel: 613-224-8072
102-30 Concourse Gate, Ottawa, Ontario, K2E 7V7

The Humane Society of the United States

www.hsus.org
Tel: 202-452-1100
2100 L St, NW Washington, DC 20037

BEHAVIOURAL PROBLEMS

If you are experiencing behavioural problems with your cat, it is best to get help fast before habits become too established. Look for someone with both practical experience and academic knowledge. They should work on veterinary referral, and be insured. Contact the following organizations or ask your vet to refer you to someone they trust:

The International Association of Animal Behavior Consultants

www.iaabc.org
Tel: 484-843-1091
565 Callery Road, Cranberry Township, PA 16066

Animal Behavior Society

http://www.animalbehavior.org/

OTHER INFORMATION

Both the Cat Fanciers' Association in the US and the Canadian Cat Association are registration bodies for the breeding and showing of pedigree cats.

Cat Fanciers' Association

www.cfainc.org
Tel: 330-680-4070
The Cat Fanciers' Association, Inc., 260 East Main Street, Alliance, OH 44601

Canadian Cat Association

www.cfainc.org
Tel: 330-680-4070
The Cat Fanciers' Association, Inc., 260 East Main Street, Alliance, OH 44601

Index

Acknowledgments

Dorling Kindersley would like to thank the following: Alice Bowden for proofreading and Margaret McCormack for the index. Niyati Gosain and Ranjita Bhattacharji for design assistance and Vibha Malhotra, Alexandra Beeden, Henry Fry, Alison Sturgeon, and Miezan van Zyl for editorial assistance. Ben Bennett, Clare Hogston, Alison and Anna Logan and Lynsey Williams at Colne Valley Veterinary Practice, Colchester; Candice Hodge and Melissa Cliffe at Posh Pet Parlour, Weybridge, for the grooming photography; and everyone who allowed their cats to be photographed: Keith Bossard (Beth), Melissa Cliffe (Rocky), Mr and Mrs Cox (Hobo), Anna Hall (Tabs and Misty), Emma Harding (Daisy), Jane Harding (Lolly), Xanthe Hodgkinson (Daisy), Rachael Parfitt-Hunt (Marvin), Helen Spencer (Harri), Antony Vernan (Milo), John Wedderburn (Lulu and Monty).

PICTURE CREDITS
The publisher would like to thank the following for their kind permission to reproduce their photographs:
l=left, r=right, t=top, c=centre, a=above, b=below.

1 Alamy Images: Blickwinkel / McPhoto / Lay. **2-3 Alamy Images:** Natalya Onishchenko. **4-5 Photoshot:** Juniors Tierbildarchiv. **4 Dreamstime.com:** Photowitch (bc). **5 Alamy Images:** Juniors Bildarchiv GmbH (bl). **Getty Images:** -Oxford- / E+ (bc). **6 Alamy Images:** Juniors Bildarchiv GmbH (tl). **Corbis:** (tr). **SuperStock:** Biosphoto (tc). **7 Alamy Images:** Graham Jepson (tl); Juniors Bildarchiv GmbH (tr). **Getty Images:** Cindy Prins / Flickr (tc). **8-9 Dreamstime.com:** Photowitch. **9 Alamy Images:** Juniors Bildarchiv GmbH (ca). **Corbis:** Image Source (cb). **10 Dreamstime.com:** Qqzoe (bl). **11 Alamy Images:** Jankurnelius (bc). **12 Corbis:** D. Sheldon / F1 Online (cra). **Dreamstime.com:** Victoria Purdie (bl). **13 Alamy Images:** Jerónimo Alba (tr). **16 Alamy Images:** Juniors Bildarchiv GmbH (bl). **Dreamstime.com:** Gkamov (cla). **18 Dreamstime.com:** Stuart Key (ca). **20 Alamy Images:** Isobel Flynn (crb); Tierfotoagentur / R. Richter (cr). **21 Corbis:** Image Source (tl). **Getty Images:** Vstock LLC (br). **22 Alamy Images:** Juniors Bildarchiv GmbH (crb). **23 Corbis:** Mitsuaki Iwago / Minden Pictures (tl). **25 Alamy Images:** Isobel Flynn (ca). **Getty Images:** Les Hirondelles Photography / Flickr (cb). **26 Alamy Images:** Juniors Bildarchiv GmbH (bl). **Dreamstime.com:** Llareggub (crb). **27 Dreamstime.com:** Zoran Milutinovic (tr). **28 Alamy Images:** Juniors Bildarchiv GmbH (br). **29 Corbis:** Splash News (tl). **30 Alamy Images:** Ovia Images (bl). **Getty Images:** Cindy Prins / Flickr (ca). **36 Alamy Images:** Juniors Bildarchiv GmbH (bl). **SuperStock:** Juniors (crb). **37 Alamy Images:** Juniors Bildarchiv GmbH (tl). **38 Alamy Images:** Brigette Sullivan / Outer Focus Photos (br). **Getty Images:** Les Hirondelles Photography / Flickr (bl). **39 Alamy Images:** Juniors Bildarchiv GmbH (cla, tr). **40-41 Alamy Images:** Juniors Bildarchiv GmbH. **41 Alamy Images:** Tierfotoagentur / R. Richter (ca). **Getty Images:** Akimasa Harada / Flickr (cb). **44 Alamy Images:** Graham Jepson (cla). **46 Alamy Images:** Petra Wegner (bl). **Getty Images:** Liz Whitaker / Flickr (crb). **50 Alamy Images:** FB-StockPhoto (bl). **51 Alamy Images:** Angela Hampton Picture Library (tl). **Getty Images:** GK Hart / Vikki Hart / The Image Bank (tr). **52 Alamy Images:** Nigel Cattlin (bc). **Corbis:** Bill Beatty / Visuals Unlimited (fbr); Dennis Kunkel Microscopy, Inc. / Visuals Unlimited (br). **53 Alamy Images:** Andrew Robinson (cra). **55 Alamy Images:** Keith Mindham (bl). **Dorling Kindersley:** Kitten courtesy of Betty (tr). **56 Dreamstime.com:** Brenda Carson (crb); Teodororoianu (bl). **57 Alamy Images:** Tierfotoagentur / R. Richter (tr). **58 Alamy Images:** Juniors Bildarchiv GmbH (cra). **60 Alamy Images:** Juniors Bildarchiv GmbH (cra). **Dreamstime.com:** Tyler Olson (bl). **61 Dreamstime.com:** Hellem (cra); Kati Molin (bl). **62 Alamy Images:** Petra Wegner (bl). **63 Alamy Images:** Juniors Bildarchiv GmbH (tl). **Corbis:** Julian Winslow / ableimages (cra). **64 Alamy Images:** Blickwinkel / Mcphoto / Lay (b). **66 Getty Images:** Kin Ming Ho / Flickr (bl). **67 Alamy Images:** Carola Schubbel / Zoonar GmbH (clb). **Getty Images:** Konrad Wothe (cra). **69 FLPA:** Chris Brignell (c). **70 Getty Images:** Akimasa Harada / Flickr (bl). **71 Alamy Images:** Gregory Preest (tl). **Fotolia:** Urso Antonio (bl). **72-73 Getty Images:** -Oxford- / E+. **73 Alamy Images:** Denise Hager / Catchlight Visual Services (ca). **74 Fotolia:** Kirill Kedrinski (bl). **75 Alamy Images:** Brian Hoffman (bl). **Dreamstime.com:** Printmore (cla); Taviphoto (ca). **76 Alamy Images:** Denise Hager / Catchlight Visual Services (bl). **77 SuperStock:** Biosphoto (cl). **78 Getty Images:** Cindy Prins / Flickr Open (br). **79 Alamy Images:** Angela Hampton Picture Library (tr). **81 Getty Images:** David & Micha Sheldon / F1online (cb). **82 Alamy Images:** Juniors Bildarchiv GmbH (clb). **Photoshot:** Juniors Tierbildarchiv (br). **85 SuperStock:** Juniors (t). **87 123RF.com:** Anna Yakimova (tl).

All other images © Dorling Kindersley
For further information see:
www.dkimages.com